FINANCIAL PLANNING AND MONITORING

Advanced GNVQ

FINANCIAL PLANNING AND MONITORING

Advanced GNVQ

Karl Smith

PITMAN PUBLISHING
128 Long Acre, London WC2E 9AN

A Division of Pearson Professional Limited

First published in Great Britain 1995

© Karl Smith 1995

A CIP catalogue record for this book can be obtained from the British Library.

ISBN 0 273 60567 4

10 9 8 7 6 5 4 3 2 1

Typeset by M Rules
Printed and bound in Great Britain by Clays Ltd, St Ives plc.

The Publishers' policy is to use paper manufactured from sustainable forests.

Contents

Element 11.4
INVESTIGATE HOW ORGANISATIONS USE FINANCIAL INFORMATION TO ASSESS PERFORMANCE AND MAKE DECISIONS

Acknowledgements

I would like to thank the staff of Pitman Publishing for their help in producing this book, particularly Ian Little and Wendy Brown. I would also like to thank Llandrillo College for being able to reprint part of the College plan.

Karl Smith

Note to the user

To assist the student and lecturer in using this text, the performance criteria for each unit and core skill are referenced in the margin where relevant. The reference may extend over a single paragraph or a few pages.

The abbreviations used are as follows:

PC   Unit Performance Criteria

Core Skill Performance Criteria:

AN   Application of Number

C   Communication

IT   Information Technology

Element 11.1

EXPLAIN THE NEED FOR FINANCIAL INFORMATION AS PART OF BUSINESS PLANNING AND MONITORING

PERFORMANCE CRITERIA

1 **The financial inputs in a range of business plans are identified and described**
   Range: corporate staffing and operational plans, sources of financial
            information internally/externally generated and their limitations

2 **The role of financial information in business decision-making is identified and explained**
   Range: evaluation, measurement; short-, medium-, long-term; operational,
            strategic

3 **The responsibilities of financial management and the nature of relationships with other functions/departments are investigated**
   Range: typical organisation structure, plan of financial management in the
            structure, typical job descriptions, likely membership of committees,
            advisory and line responsibilities

EVIDENCE INDICATORS

The preparation of a report based on a comparison of local organisations
indicating role of financial management. Common responsibilities and
involvement in planning and monitoring activity identified.

1 Financial planning

> 'Annual income twenty pounds, annual expenditure nineteen pounds nineteen and six, result happiness. Annual income twenty pounds, annual expenditure twenty pounds and sixpence, result misery.'
>
> Mr Micawber in *David Copperfield*, by Charles Dickens

Mr Micawber understood intuitively what some managers sadly never realise: the success (or 'happiness') of any organisation relies on managing finances effectively.

Business is concerned with money. There are two sides to the money-making process: money comes in, usually through sales, and money leaves, through costs and expenses. Financial planning and monitoring concerns itself with both sides of this process.

In this book we are primarily concerned with providing information for managers of the business. While other people and organisations may be interested in the information, financial planning and monitoring is first and foremost a decision-making tool. This means that the areas covered are essentially **internal** in their usage. Indeed, in some instances the information is secret, and would have a serious effect on the business if disclosed to a competitor.

ACTIVITY

Produce a list of other people and organisations who might be interested in the financial planning of a particular business, and identify the type of information useful to them.

Financial planning is concerned with:

- how much money is coming into and out of the organisation
- when the money comes in and goes out
- how to reduce the level of money leaving the organisation

Financial monitoring involves the recording and measuring of financial aspects of the business on a regular basis. This observing, or monitoring, provides management with information that is used to help in planning.

Throughout this book, we shall be looking mainly at the costs side of the organisation – how it is measured, analysed and controlled. The reader should be aware that costs are closely associated with the other side of the business – money coming in through sales. Costs, as we shall see, influence what is sold, how much of it is sold, and at what price.

It is important to remember that the costing and planning systems covered in this book may not be undertaken by all organisations. There is always a trade-off between the usefulness of information and the cost of collecting it. Information that does not help an organisation achieve its goals can serve merely to distract management from their job.

PC 2 Why organisations plan

A plan is a **future projection**. It shows where the organisation is going in the future. The better the plan, the less risk there is of the organisation going out of business. It is fair to say that all businesses and organisations (whether profit-making or not) undertake some form of financial planning, however basic. How well this is done often determines whether a business is a success or failure. Several thousand business failures each year testify to the fact that the benefits of planning are not as widely appreciated as they could be.

Planning provides useful information for several groups:

- investors in the business
- lenders of money to the business
- managers of the business
- government agencies such as Inland Revenue and Customs and Excise

The benefits of planning can be summarised as follows:

1. *Efficiency*. Planning can save time and money. Thinking things through can prevent potentially wasteful spending occurring.
2. *Control*. The well-planned organisation anticipates changes rather than merely reacting to events, or 'fire-fighting' as it is sometimes known.
3. *Resource allocation*. Capital expenditure can be made in areas that will earn the most money for the business. This consideration applies equally to non-profit-making organisations.
4. *Persuasion*. Businesses need to persuade banks to lend money to them, and shareholders to invest in them. Well thought out plans persuade people that the business knows what it is doing.

■ The planning cycle

Planning consists of three stages, which can be regarded as a cycle, as shown in Fig. 1.1

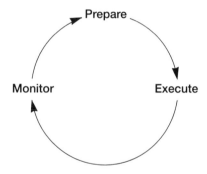

Fig. 1.1   The planning cycle

Preparing the plan involves creating a workable plan. This is usually the most time-consuming aspect of planning. Many people may be involved at this stage.

Executing the plan occurs when the plan is put into practice. This may happen immediately, or there may be a gap between preparing and executing the plan. For example, a business may plan to invest heavily in training the workforce. However, the increased spending might not occur until the start of the new financial year, when a new budget is available to spend.

ACTIVITY

Why do you think it is important that the time between preparing and executing a plan is kept as short as possible?

Monitoring the plan is the third stage in the planning cycle. What is actually happening is compared with what was meant to happen in the plan.

For example:

A bus company has planned to run its buses with an average 75 per cent of seats occupied on each journey. After three months, monitoring shows that the actual occupancy is 64 per cent. With this information, management can now try to find ways to achieve the original planned 75 per cent.

Sometimes, the original plan may be unrealistic; it might have been badly thought out, or something may have changed outside the control of the organisation. Using the bus company as an example again, their fares might have been based on low petrol prices. If the price of petrol suddenly increases, the original plan will be inaccurate.

In either case, the plan will not match what is actually happening – monitoring will soon show this. The results of the monitoring can be used to alter the original plan or create a new one.

Strategic plan

The first stage of the planning process is the strategic plan. This takes a long-term look at the future of the organisation, and considers possible major changes of structure, goals or direction.

Annual operating plan

This involves more detailed figures, and is sometimes known as the **master budget**. It is covered in more detail in Element 11.2 of this book.

Modified plan

The annual plan may need to be modified if circumstances change. For example, if sales of a product are much higher than expected, the business may devote more time and money to producing it. Existing plans will therefore need to be altered.

Forecast

These occur at the end of the financial year, and are the basis on which next year's plans are made. They can also occur at any stage through the year, to predict what will happen in the rest of the year. Obviously, the nearer the forecast is made to the end of the year, the more accurate it is likely to be.

The financial plan – a comprehensive example

A financial plan is only one of the plans an organisation might make. All plans should be designed to help the organisation achieve its goals. The example given here is for a non-profit making organisation, Llandrillo College in North Wales. The college's goals are set out in a **mission statement**:

To establish the college as a centre of excellence, innovation and a community resource which provides comprehensive education and training.

To achieve this, the college has several **strategic aims:**

Within the period of this plan, we shall aim to:

- *achieve planned levels of growth*
- *improve quality and service to clients*
- *continue the improvement of the existing college sites and further develop physical and learning resources*
- *encourage and support entrepreneurial and commercial activity and extend the services offered to local businesses*

The strategic plan is divided into the following sections:

- students and provision
- quality
- human resources
- physical resources
- finance
- systems
- sensitivity analysis

Looking at the financial plan in more detail, the aims include:

- efficiency gains which offset enhanced levels of funding
- enhanced levels of expenditure on premises
- increasing levels of 'financial support' to enable students to participate

There are financial implications to all the plans. For example, the human resources plan calls for more staff training – this costs money. We will now look in detail at one of the plans:

PHYSICAL RESOURCES

Action	By whom/date	Resource implications	Review
Prepare detailed planning application to support new library and resources block – July 1994. Performing arts – July 1995.	AP Finance Estates mgr JULY 1994	£1 000 000 £750 000	Building committee
Carry out feasibility study on further development of an outreach site.	Head of Academic Development AP Finance SEPT 1994	£300 000 estd.	Building committee, Finance and Policy Committee
Carry out full inventory of physical resources to assist in development of fixed asset register.	Asst Director Finance JULY 1994	£1000	Principal

Cost centres

Cost centres are 'collecting places' for costs. All costs are sent to a particular cost centre. These cost centres can be:

- departments, such as maintenance department or stores department
- other service areas, such as the staff canteen

- other groups of expenses e.g. a building. In this case, items such as rent, rates, and repairs associated with the building will be grouped together.

Cost centres serve two main purposes:

1. To aid cost control by attributing all costs to a specific centre.
2. To improve staff accountability by having a member of staff responsible for each cost centre.

Below is an example of a cost centre within a large organisation (based on a real-life company):

Chiptech PLC is a large company making electronic chips and components.

The testing division tests products from each of 14 different production divisions within the organisation. In an attempt to improve cost efficiency, the testing division becomes a separate **cost centre**.

The testing division now charges the other divisions at **full cost** for its services (**direct costs** plus a share of **overheads**). However, the other divisions are now free to buy testing services from outside the organisation – they no longer have to rely on Chiptech PLC's own testing division.

(The cost terms in bold are referred to in later chapters – don't worry if they seem strange at this stage.)

ACTIVITY

PC 1
PC 2

Why do you think Chiptech PLC established the testing division as a separate cost centre? Why are the other divisions now able to buy testing services in from outside companies?

ACTIVITY

PC 1

Find out what the cost centres are for your organisation or college. Are they departments, or other types of cost centre?

Revenue centres

These are similar to cost centres, except that they are collecting places for money coming *in* to the organisation. For example, a large business with several different sales regions may classify each sales region as a separate revenue centre.

Profit centres

Where a division of an organisation is responsible for both income (revenue) and expenditure (costs), it is possible to calculate how much **profit** that division has made. In a large college, the Business Studies Department may be a separate profit centre, so that it is responsible for costs, such as staff wages, and generating income by attracting students.

Both revenue centres and profit centres have the same purpose as cost centres: control and accountability. Some costs (or revenue) are easier to attribute to a particular centre than others. To understand this, look at the following example:

Xtreme Ltd make skiwear. The company is split into three manufacturing divisions: Jackets, Trousers and Accessories. All divisions are located in the same factory. Each division is a separate cost centre.

The following costs occur:

- factory rent
- general office staff wages
- machinists' wages
- sales staff wages
- heating and lighting
- raw materials

ACTIVITY

Looking at the list of expenses, say which you think would be
(i) easy
(ii) difficult
to send to a particular cost centre.

Do you think the company could reorganise the cost centres to make this
task easier?

SUMMARY

1 **There is a trade-off between the value of information and the cost
of getting that information.**

2 **A plan is a future projection.**

3 **Planning is very important to the successful running of an
organisation.**

4 **The planning cycle consists of three stages: preparation, monitoring
and execution.**

5 **A strategic plan looks at the long-term future of the organisation.**

6 **An operational (operating) plan looks at the next year.**

7 **A financial plan is only one of several plans an organisation makes.**

8 **Cost centres are collecting places for costs.**

9 **Cost centres aid cost control and improve staff accountability.**

FURTHER ACTIVITY

PC 2

(i) Find out what the goals of your organisation or college are. Obtain a copy
of the mission statement if one exists.
(ii) Obtain a mission statement or equivalent for a profit-making business and
compare the stated intentions with that of the college.

2 Responsibilities for financial planning and monitoring

PC 3

Which people within an organisation are concerned with financial planning? They can be divided into three broad categories:

1. Those who manage the broad policies of the organisation.
2. Those who manage sections of the organisation.
3. Those who are responsible for daily operation of the organisation.

The first category will include:

- directors (executive and non-executive)
- trustees (of a charitable organisation)
- governors and chief executive (such as schools and colleges)

The second category will include:

- sales manager
- marketing manager
- production manager
- chief accountant
- departmental managers

The third category will include:

- buyers
- sales staff
- production workers
- production supervisors
- planners

A typical organisation chart for those involved in financial planning and monitoring is shown in Fig. 2.1.

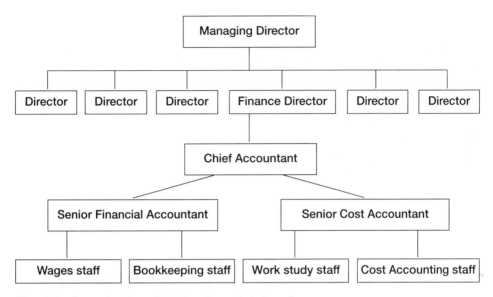

Fig. 2.1 Organisation chart for financial planning

All the personnel within a company or organisation should be working towards the same goals. It is important, therefore, that the organisation structure is not too rigid. For example, a company that designs and makes products will need input from designers into the financial planning process. Although not accountants, such people can greatly aid management in producing realistic targets and estimates.

The planning process and staff

A key rule in financial planning is to involve as many staff as possible. The following people should *always* be consulted:

1 **Departmental managers.** Such people often have a broader view of the organisation's goals, problems and situation than do shopfloor workers. It is also possible that they may have encountered similar situations before: in such a case, their experience will be invaluable in assessing plans.
2 **Supervisors.** As people responsible for dealing directly with the workforce, their objectives may not be the same as those of the financial planners. It is important to find what their views are. In particular, how much autonomy do the supervisors want? How much financial freedom are the supervisors capable of dealing with?

3 **The rest of the workforce.** Good ideas are not restricted to senior management. Many workers come up with ideas which, if implemented, could benefit the organisation enormously. It is a pity that more organisations do not realise the benefits of listening to their workforce.

■ Planning and motivation

Involving people in planning helps them feel a part of the process, and makes them more inclined to help implement the planning decisions made. The industrial psychologist Fred Herzberg states in his theory of motivation that giving people responsibility is a strong motivating factor. Being in charge of an area of work that is recognisably 'yours' encourages you to perform well.

C 3.1

ACTIVITY

Can you think of a situation in your organisation where good ideas have been taken up by management? What were the successes arising from this? Are there any examples of good ideas *not* being adopted by management? Discuss these in a group.

Levels of control

A financial plan for an organisation may be made up of several parts. Some parts of the plan may be more important than others. From this, it is essential that the right person is responsible for each particular part of the financial plan. The more important the part of the plan, the more senior should be the person responsible for it:

The higher the level of control needed, the higher the manager needed.

For example:

Budgeted profit and loss account for year ended 31 x 19xx

	£	Controlled by:
Sales	20 000	Sales manager
Cost of sales	13 000	Chief buyer
Gross profit	7 000	
less:		
Wages	3 000	Personnel manager
Office overheads	1 400	Office manager
Net profit	2 600	Managing director

The various elements of the financial plan (in this case a budgeted profit and loss account) are controlled by a particular manager. The most important, highest level figure is net profit. This needs the highest level of control, so it is the responsibility of the managing director.

The office overheads budget is the overall responsibility of the office manager. Within that budget, there will be smaller budgets requiring a lower level of control, such as:

	£	Responsibility
Repairs	700	Maintenance officer
Photocopying	250	Secretary
Stationery	320	Secretary
Telephone calls	130	Deputy office manager
	1400	

Lines of control

A **line of control** shows who is responsible to who within the organisation. This can be determined by looking at an organisation chart.

For example, the line of control for a trainee accounts clerk in the costing department of a company might look like Fig. 2.2.

A danger with any systems-based approach to problem solving lies in ignoring the human behaviour element. By not taking into account the wishes, feelings and opinions of the workforce, a system is likely to fail. Even the best system requires people to implement it. Financial planning

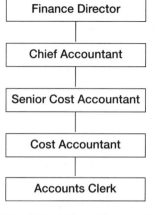

```
┌─────────────────────────┐
│     Finance Director     │
└─────────────────────────┘
             │
┌─────────────────────────┐
│    Chief Accountant      │
└─────────────────────────┘
             │
┌─────────────────────────┐
│  Senior Cost Accountant  │
└─────────────────────────┘
             │
┌─────────────────────────┐
│     Cost Accountant      │
└─────────────────────────┘
             │
┌─────────────────────────┐
│     Accounts Clerk       │
└─────────────────────────┘
```

Fig. 2.2 Lines of control

and monitoring, when done well, attempts to take account of the human element in the system. Accountants are often criticised for being 'number obsessed' and ignoring the human element; as you progress through this book, notice that the human factor *is* considered.

PC 2
PC 3
C 3.1

ACTIVITY

In a group, discuss any examples you have encountered in the workplace of:

● a new system being introduced
● the reaction of staff to the new system

Say what you think are the reasons for staff reaction.

■ The staffing plan

In order to ensure that lines of control exist, and are effective, an organisation needs to have a **staffing plan**. Such a plan will include:

● the number of staff needed
● the type of staff needed (expertise and skills)
● individual responsibilities and duties
● line responsibilities
● structure of working teams

This is an essential part of any organisation's planning. Without proper consideration of staffing, the organisation will not function effectively.

The financial aspect of the staffing plan is dealt with in the **staffing budget**. This is covered in more detail in the chapters on budgets.

SUMMARY

1   The people concerned with financial planning within an organisation can be divided into three categories.

2   The first category includes directors; the second category includes managers; the third category includes lower level workers.

3   Too rigid an organisation structure prevents full consultation in financial planning.

4   Involving staff in planning can improve morale and aid motivation.

5   The higher the level of control, the more senior the manager needed.

6   Lines of control show who is responsible to whom in an organisation.

7   Planning systems need to take into account the human element.

FURTHER ACTIVITY

PC 3
C 3.1

In a group, discuss to what extent shopfloor workers should be involved in producing complex financial plans for a company.

Element 11.1 Assignment

Select two local organisations. Working in groups, for each organisation:

PC 3
C 3.1
C 3.2
C 3.3
IT 3.1
IT 3.2
IT 3.3
IT 3.4

Task 1

Produce an organisation chart showing the people who work in the financial department. Compare the two organisation charts, highlighting any difference in structure.

PC 1
PC 2
PC 3
C 3.1
C 3.2
C 3.3
IT 3.1
IT 3.2
IT 3.3
IT 3.4

Task 2

Find out who has responsibility for various areas of income or expenditure. Produce a chart showing the various cost centres (or budgets), and how they are linked.

Task 3

For one of the people mentioned in Task 2, find out what financial information he or she finds useful for this particular job.

Element 11.2

EXPLAIN AND ILLUSTRATE THE KEY FEATURES OF A BUDGETARY PLANNING SYSTEM

PERFORMANCE CRITERIA

1 **Types of budget are identified and described**
   Range: master, sales, product, staffing

2 **The structure of budgets is demonstrated**
   Range: elements, expense heads, responsibilities, budget period and
   subdivision into reporting periods

3 **Procedures for compilation of budgets are specified**
   Range: budget committee, co-ordination between functions/departments,
   identification of constraints

4 **Different monitoring arrangements used by organisations are
   compared**
   Range: variance analysis, exception reporting, frequency and arrangements:
   timing of reporting

EVIDENCE INDICATORS

   The preparation of a sales budget using actual documentation and
   information on related activities. This should include a discussion of
   significant differences from budget.

3 Budgets – an introduction

Budgets are an important part of financial planning. A good business needs to **plan ahead**: without knowing what costs to expect, or how many items of a product you expect to sell, it is very difficult to operate efficiently.

Most people plan ahead for events such as holidays or getting married – without the planning, things would not run as smoothly! Businesses are no different – adequate planning is essential to their running.

Budgets are familiar features of public sector organisations such as local councils. The best-known budget is the one produced by the government, which predicts all the money which the government will receive and spend during the next financial year.

> A budget is a **detailed plan for a future period of time.** It may be a plan for the next twelve months, ten years, or just the next week; it can be a short- or long-term plan.

All budgets are **expressed in numbers (usually pounds)**. Most of us are familiar with the idea of 'operating within a budget' – only having a set amount to spend. When the budget is spent, there is no more money left. There are many more types of budgets, however.

An example of a budget which is expressed in numbers but *not* pounds is a **production budget.** A manufacturing company might plan the number of items of a product it will make:

Hercules Ltd

Production budget for 19X4

	Jan	Feb	Mar	Apr . . . etc.
No. of units	90	100	120	80

Notice that this budget says how many units Hercules Ltd plan to make – it doesn't mention cost at all.

Strategic planning

Some businesses think several years ahead, and may set long-term budgets. Such long-term thinking considers areas such as product development, expansion overseas, or changing the business structure. This process is known as **strategic planning**, and most large businesses do this in some form or other. Budgets put figures to these plans, and can help in deciding whether the plan is a good idea. Also, budgets help in their implementation. For example, a business that currently buys components from a supplier decides to produce the component itself. This means opening a factory, equipping it and training staff in advance. Budgets will set aside money for doing this.

ACTIVITY

Can you think of the
(i) advantages
(ii) difficulties
in producing long-term budgets?

■ The uses of budgets

The five main uses of budgets can be summarised as follows:

- planning
- control
- implementation
- monitoring and reviewing
- motivation

Planning

By knowing what to expect, progress is made much easier. For example, if it is thought that there will be a greatly increased demand for a product, a company can plan purchase of new machines, training more staff, or buying a bigger factory.

Control

By restricting the size of the budget given to a department or section, the business can keep control of expenditure. Without the budget to limit spending, a department could easily spend money on unnecessary items. If you do not believe this, think of a computer department in your school or college. Look at what equipment there is, and make a shopping list of the very best available. Now think how much your shopping list would cost!

Implementation

The budget process forces managers to look carefully at what their costs or usage of machines and materials are. By allocating budgets of different sizes to different areas of operation, a business can determine the direction in which it is heading. If a chemical business wants to develop new 'green' products, it may give an increased budget to its research and development department.

Monitoring and reviewing

At the end of the budget period, actual performance can be compared with budgeted performance, to see how well (or badly) the business has done. Unless there are budget figures to compare with, a statement of costs is not very useful. This process is known as **budgetary control**. By narrowing down problems to specific budgets, it is easier to take corrective action. This does not have to wait until the end of the budget period – by checking the actual performance against budget on a monthly (or even weekly) basis, problems come to light much sooner. These can then be corrected before too much damage is done.

Motivation

Depending on how the budget is set, a budget can have an effect on people's morale in work. This aspect of budgeting will be looked at in more detail in a later chapter.

The types of budget

Big organisations may have a very large number of budgets. Some of these budgets, as we shall see, themselves depend on other budgets to be calculated. The question follows, then: with which budget does an organisation start?

For most businesses, the usual starting point is the **sales budget**.

Example of a sales budget:

Hercules Ltd

Sales Budget for the year 19X3

	Jan	Feb	Mar	Apr	May	Jun
Units	90	100	120	150	190	260
Selling price per unit:	500	500	500	500	500	500
(£000)	45	50	60	75	95	130

	Jul	Aug	Sep	Oct	Nov	Dec
Units	300	280	160	90	130	96
Selling price per unit:	500	500	500	500	500	500
(£000)	150	140	80	45	65	48

Notice that the sales budget is expressed both in units **(sales volume)** and in pounds £ **(sales value)**. There is a big difference between the two! Sales value is calculated by multiplying **sales volume** (no. of units sold) by **price per unit**.

A sales budget is the usual starting point because most other items depend upon sales, such as:

- the level of production
- raw materials budget
- cost of packaging
- number of labour hours worked
- stock levels

Looking at the first of these examples, a business is unlikely to plan the amount it will *make* of a product unless it thinks it can *sell* the product!

ACTIVITY

List as many costs as you can think of which depend on sales.

■ The production budget

This follows on from the sales budget. As seen above, this depends primarily on the expected sales. It is also affected by any change in stock level planned. Below is an example illustrating this:

Hercules Ltd expect to sell 3000 units of a product during the next year. The company has maintained a stock level of 500 units in the past, but wants to increase this to 700 units by the year end. What is the production budget?

Production required   = sales + increase in stock level
                            = 3000 + (700 − 500)
Production budget   = 3200 units

ACTIVITY

Notice that the budget is expressed in units. What additional information would you need to show the production budget in pounds?

ACTIVITY

Robertson PLC make industrial heaters. Their sales budget for the next 12 months is 34 000 units. The current stock level is 2850 units. Their policy is to increase stock levels to 10 per cent of the year's sales by the year end.

What is the production budget for the next 12 months?

Once the production budget is established, several other budgets can be produced. These include:

- materials usage budget
- machine utilisation budget
- labour (wages) budget

Materials usage budget

This budget estimates the amounts of raw material that will be used during the budget period. It is very important in some industries, where raw materials are difficult to get hold of. Failing to have the necessary raw material will stop production – budgeting helps prevent this.

Starlight Ltd make two products: Bugs and Ticks

| Each Bug requires: | 2 kilos material A |
| | 1.5 kilos material B |

| Each Tick requires: | 0.5 kilos material A |
| | 5 kilos material B |

| The Production budget is: | Bugs 3000 |
| | Ticks 5000 |

The materials usage budget will look like this:

		Material A	Material B
Required for production:			
Bugs	(3000 × 2 kilos)	6000	
	(3000 × 1.5 kilos)		4 500
Ticks	(5000 × 0.5 kilos)	2500	
	(5000 × 5 kilos)		25 000
		8500 kilos	29 500 kilos

Note that this budget is expressed in kilos. If the cost per kilo is: material A £4 and material B £2, the cost of materials used is:

material A   £34 000
material B   £59 000

Machine utilisation budget

This budget estimates the number of hours each machine will be used. By knowing this, a business can also estimate what the likely repair and maintenance bills will be. More importantly, this is very useful where there is only a limited amount of machinery. If several different products are being made, we need to know how much machine time each product uses. Without knowing this, we cannot plan the most efficient use of machine time. (This idea is looked at in more detail in a later chapter.) For example:

Each Bug takes: 6 hrs on machine X
                    2 hrs on machine Z
Each Tick takes: 1 hr on machine X
                    3 hrs on machine Z

Machine utilisation budget

	Machine X Hrs per unit		Machine Z Hrs per unit	
Bug (3000 units)	6	18 000	2	6 000
Tick (5000 units)	1	5 000	3	15 000
Total hours:		23 000		21 000

■ Labour (wages) budget

This expresses the number of hours needed to meet required output. In an industry where skilled labour is needed, the labour budget helps predict whether new staff need to be taken on or trained (or made redundant!). For example:

Each Bug takes: 3 hrs direct labour to make
Each Tick takes: 2 hrs direct labour to make

Labour budget

Product	Production	Hours required Hrs per unit	Total hrs	Hrly rate	Cost
Bug	3000	3	9 000	£4	£36 000
Tick	5000	2	10 000	£4	£40 000
			19 000		£76 000

Notice that total hours required are 19 000. If the labour costs £4 per hour (i.e. hourly rate), multiplying total hours by hourly rate gives cost.

The above are the main budgets associated with production. To see how they are all linked, look at the following comprehensive example:

Ozymandias Ltd make two products: Wands and Cauldrons. The following information is available:

	Wands	Cauldrons
Estimated sales	600	750
Selling price	£17	£24
Current stocks	100	140
Desired stock level at end of year	125	110

Materials usage:

	Wands	Cauldrons
Material D	10 kilos	2.5 kilos
Material F	4 kilos	7 kilos

Machine usage:

	Wands	Cauldrons
lathe	3 hrs	2 hrs
grinder	1 hr	3.5 hrs
polisher	4 hrs	1.2 hrs
Labour hours:	3	4.5

Labour hourly rate = £3.50

Sales budget

	Sales(volume)	Selling price	Sales value
Wands	600	£17	£10 200
Cauldrons	750	£24	£18 000
			£28 200

Production budget

	Wands	Cauldrons
Sales	600	750
Increase/(decrease) in stocks	25	(30)
Production requirement	625	720

Materials usage budget

		Material D	Material F
Required for production:			
Wands	(625 × 10 kilos)	6250	
	(625 × 4 kilos)		2500
Cauldrons	(720 × 2.5 kilos)	1800	
	(720 × 7 kilos)		5040
		8050	7540

Machine usage budget

Product	Units	Hrs/unit	Lathe	Hrs/unit	Grinder	Hrs/unit	Polisher
Wand	625	3	1875	1	625	4	2500
Cauldron	720	2	1440	3.5	2520	1.2	864
			3315		3145		3364

Labour budget

Product	Production	Hours required Hrs per unit	Total hrs	Hrly rate	Cost
Wands	625	3	1875	£3.50	£6 562.50
Cauldrons	720	4.5	3240	£3.50	£11 340.00
					£17 902.50

■ Staffing budget

Not all organisations make things. In businesses which provide a service, or in government organisations, staff costs are often the single biggest cost. For example, in schools and colleges, staff wages account for 70 to 80 per cent of all costs. It is very important, therefore, that staffing costs are controlled.

A staffing budget depends on two things:

- how many staff
- how much the staff are paid

AN 3.2

ACTIVITY

What might happen if a service organisation set its staffing budget too low?

■ Cash budget

This budget is also known as a **cash flow forecast**. It is usually constructed for a 12-month period or longer, and shows the amount of ready cash in the business for each month. It is calculated by estimating the cash inflows and outflows for each month. This cannot be done until all other budgets (except the master budget) have been produced.

Cash is the life blood of most businesses, and lack of cash is the main reason for firms collapsing. A cash budget is essential if a business wants to borrow money, as it gives the bank an indication of whether the loan can be paid back. A detailed coverage of cash budgets is outside the scope of this unit, but the subject is fully covered in other GNVQ units.

■ Master budget

The master budget involves the production of a forecast **profit and loss account** and **balance sheet**. As such, it is the final stage in the budgeting process, bringing together all the other budgets.

The relationship between budgets can be illustrated in a simple 'family tree' shown in Fig. 3.1.

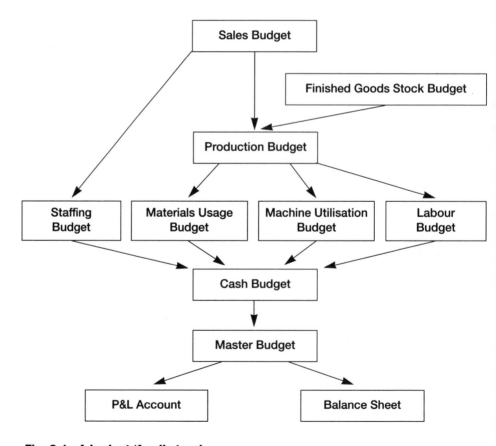

Fig. 3.1 A budget 'family tree'

SUMMARY

1 Budgets are detailed plans for the future, and are expressed in numbers.

2 Strategic planning involves planning for long-term changes within an organisation.

3 There are five main reasons for having budgets: planning; control; implementation; monitoring and evaluating; motivating staff.

4 The sales budget is the usual starting point in preparing budgets. It can be expressed in terms of value (£) or volume (number of units sold).

5 The production budget depends on expected sales and stock levels.

6 Other production dependent budgets are: raw materials usage budget; labour budget; machine utilisation budget.

7 The master budget brings together all other budgets, and is used to produce forecast final accounts.

4 Preparing a budget

The success or otherwise of the entire budgeting exercise for an organisation depends on how well budgets are prepared. This chapter looks at the various stages of preparing (or setting) a budget.

Stage 1: Appointing the people responsible for preparing a budget

■ The budget controller

Someone with the overall responsibility of preparing budgets needs to be appointed. This person is known as the **budget controller**, or **budget officer**. This is a senior position within the organisation. The person appointed needs to be good with figures (usually an accountant), but should also have a good understanding of the technical side of the business. In a manufacturing company, this means having someone who understands the various stages of the production process.

■ The budget committee

The make-up of the budget committee varies according to the company, but generally it will include:

- the managing director
- the finance director
- the sales director

- the production manager
- departmental managers

The role of the budget committee is a three-stage one:

1. submit initial budget proposals
2. discuss these proposals
3. approve the final budget figures

The budget committee should meet regularly (at least once a month) to discuss budgets. It should be noted that the budget committee does not only set new budgets – it looks at existing budgets and compares with actual figures: the committee has a monitoring role.

Stage 2: Liaising with budget managers

While the budget committee may have the power to decide the final budget figures, it is important to consult those who have to work with a particular budget.

For example, a machine usage budget will require detailed technical knowledge: how long each unit takes to make on a particular machine; whether any machine needs repair or replacement; whether enough staff are trained to use the machine to its full capacity. Clearly, to arrive at sensible budget figures, the committee will have to discuss with foremen and machine operators.

In addition, the person who will be in overall charge of a particular budget will need to be involved in discussions. This person is likely to have a broader knowledge of budget requirements than, for example, a foreman or machine operator. The person who has responsibility for a particular budget is known as a **budget manager**. Each budget produced will have its own budget manager.

In organisations which use cost centres, each budget will be attached to a particular cost centre. The budget manager is usually the cost centre manager. (Where there are smaller budgets within a cost centre, other staff may be budget managers.)

ACTIVITY

What are the advantages of having a separate budget manager for each budget?

ACTIVITY

For your own organisation or college, find out who is in charge of a budget. Is the person also a cost centre manager?

A further reason for involving the budget managers is that of **morale**. Budgets that managers feel they have a hand in compiling will make them happier than budgets imposed from above. As their co-operation is vital in ensuring success, this psychological aspect of the budget process should not be ignored.

Stage 3: Comparing with previous budgets

It makes obvious sense to compare the budget being prepared with previous budgets. These will give a useful yardstick. Often producing the new budget will simply be a matter of using the most recent budget, and adding in a few minor adjustments.

Points that will need to be considered are:

- expected growth (or decline) in output
- the inflation rate
- expected efficiency gains

ACTIVITY

These are just examples of points to consider. Can you think of any others?

Example

Milligan Ltd are producing their labour budget for next year. The last budget was for £320 000.

The production level was 5000 units; this is expected to grow to 6000 units.

The production workforce are to be given a 5 per cent pay rise.

The production workforce have just received training; this should increase their productivity by 15 per cent.

What should the new labour budget be?

Answer in three stages:

(i) Current budget £320 000

Increase in production $= \dfrac{6000}{5000} = 1.2$

Higher production means more labour, so:

New budget $= £320\,000 \times 1.2$

(ii) Wage increase $= 5\%$

New budget $= (£320\,000 \times 1.2) + 5\%$
$= £403\,200$

(iii) But there has been an increase in productivity. This means less work is required per unit, **reducing** the new labour budget:

New budget $= £403\,200 - 15\%$
$= £342\,720$

Stages 2 and 3 are often reversed – the budget committee first looks at previous budgets, then seeks the advice and views of budget managers.

Stage 4: Producing the budget

Having looked at previous budgets and consulted managers and other staff, the committee can now authorise the new budget. At this stage, a final check should be made to ensure that there are no mistakes or omissions.

When all budgets are brought together to produce the **master budget**, together with budgeted profit and loss account and balance sheet, it may be necessary to revise the budgets. Clearly, if individual budgets when combined show the business makes a loss, it is sensible to look at them again!

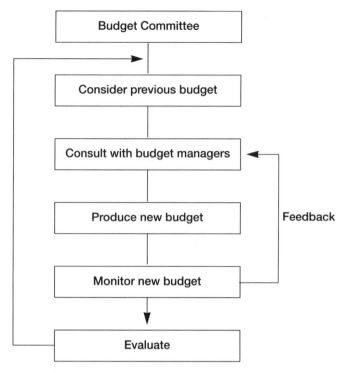

Fig. 4.1 The budgeting process

The budget committee may produce a covering report with the final budgets, explaining how these have been arrived at. The report will include comparisons with previous budgets, and notes highlighting and explaining major changes. It may also mention any recent developments, such as sales trends or raw materials price rises. The report, therefore, presents an overall picture of current trends and where the company is heading.

PC 4 Stage 5: Monitoring the budget

This very important stage, known as budgetary control, is dealt with more fully in the next chapter. Briefly, actual figures are continuously checked against budgeted figures, and any resulting difference is referred to management (and the budget committee). This can lead to subsequent modification of the original budget.

Stage 6: Evaluation

At the end of the budget period, actual performance can be reviewed against budgeted performance. The evaluation will be used as a basis for preparing the next budget.

The Sales Budget – an example

Strathglen Mineral Water Ltd sells bottled mineral water. It is a young company, and sales have expanded from Scotland and now cover most of Britain. Fiona Macleod is the sales director for the company.

As Fiona has more detailed knowledge of sales figures and prospects than anyone else in the company, she has been made responsible for compiling the sales budget.

Fiona first looks at previous years' sales figures. These are split into ten regions. Each region is under the control of a sales manager. Fiona will use the figures as a basis for estimating the forthcoming year's sales. Also, she will ask the regional sales managers whether they think sales will increase in their region (and by how much). By doing this, she is using the expertise of her sales managers, who probably know local conditions better than she does.

ACTIVITY   PC 3

Why should Fiona be careful when using the sales managers' estimates?

Fiona then needs to find information from other sources. The bottled mineral water market is growing rapidly in Britain – more people are buying the product. To find the rate of growth, Fiona looks in trade journals, the *Financial Times*, and consumer spending surveys. All of this information helps her to predict the growth in sales next year.

ACTIVITY   PC 3

Where else might Fiona Macleod look for information of this sort?

Fiona has spoken to her sales managers, read the trade papers, and confidently expects sales to grow substantially! However, Strathglen Ltd only have a small bottling plant, and she will have to check with the production manager to see if the company can meet the expected demand.

An additional problem is that sales of mineral water are seasonal: much more is sold during the summer months. Fiona sees from her estimates that the bottling plant can produce enough to satisfy most months' sales, but in July and August they cannot produce enough.

Storing the bottled water is too expensive, so Fiona has to reduce her sales estimates for July and August down to the maximum the bottling plant can produce.

PC 3

ACTIVITY

Can you think of any other factors Fiona should have considered when producing the sales budget?

Zero-based budgeting

Most budgets are produced by comparing with previous budgets. The danger of doing this is that budgets tend to go in only one direction – upwards! For example, if the staffing budget was £250 000 last year, it is tempting to think it will be at least the same, or more, next year. Wages tend to increase with inflation.

Zero-based budgeting adopts a different approach. It ignores previous budgets, starting from scratch (hence the name, 'zero-based'). The department or operation for which the budget is required is looked at in detail. Requirements are calculated and an appropriate budget is developed. Using the example of the staffing budget, zero-based budgeting would assess how many staff, and at what grade, were needed.

The advantage of this approach is that budget requirements are looked at objectively. With the traditional budget approach, people are too strongly influenced by previous budget levels. A disadvantage is that zero-rated budgeting can be time-consuming and therefore expensive to undertake. Potential savings need therefore to be weighed against the cost of undertaking the study.

The limiting budget factor

The budgeting process normally starts with the sales budget. This is because the level of sales determines all other budgets, such as production budget. Most businesses are **limited** by the sales they can make: there is no point making more of a product than can be sold. **Level of sales** is the **limiting budget factor** – other budgets can only be prepared after the sales budget.

In some cases, level of sales is *not* the limiting budget factor. Other limiting budget factors occur, often in small businesses. An example is machine hours. Where a business only has a limited amount of machinery, production cannot be increased beyond a set amount. Even if the business could sell more, it cannot because it can't produce enough goods. In this example, machine hours is the limiting budget factor. The machine hours budget needs to be prepared first, before other budgets can be prepared.

Other examples of limiting budget factors are:

- availability of raw materials
- skilled labour

ACTIVITY

Can you think of any other limiting budget factors?

PC 3

SUMMARY

1 The first stage in preparing a budget is to identify those people with overall responsibility. They will form a budget committee, which liaises with budget managers, who are in charge of specific budgets.

2 Proposed budgets are compared with previous budgets to provide a yardstick.

3 When budget managers have been consulted, and previous budgets studied, the new budgets are compiled.

4 Monitoring the budgets (known as budgetary control) occurs frequently, and provides managers with feedback.

5 Budgets are evaluated against actual performance at the end of the budget period.

6 Zero-based budgeting can prevent budgets automatically increasing from the previous year's budgets.

7 Most budgets are limited by sales. Sometimes, budgets are limited by other factors, such as available machine hours.

PC 2
AN 3.2

QUESTION

Fill in the missing gaps in the sales budget:

	Jan	Feb	Mar	Apr	May
Units	120	140	175	200	
Selling price	£3	£3	£3.25		£4
Sales value				800	900

5 Monitoring the budget

Once a budget has been approved, it is put into practice. As budgets are often for 12 months' duration, it is unwise to wait until the end of this period before comparing the actual results with budgeted figures. During that time, many changes may have occurred. The business may find itself over-producing, buying too many raw materials, or employing too many staff.

If this is so, it is essential that managers are made aware as soon as possible so that corrective action can be taken.

The difference between an actual figure and budgeted figure is known as a **variance**. A variance can be either **adverse** or **favourable**:

	Budgeted	*Actual*	*Variance*
Sales	1000 units	950 units	(50) adverse
Production	800 units	830 units	30 favourable

The process of comparing actual and budgeted figures is known as **variance analysis**. It is also used when comparing actual costs with so-called **standard costs**. (Variance analysis and standard costs are dealt with in later chapters.)

Exception reporting

It is almost certain that actual unit costs will differ in practice from budgeted costs. It is impossible to predict *exactly* what the unit cost will be.

From the management point of view, what matters is not that there is a difference; it is the *size* of the difference that is important.

The difference, or variance, should only be reported if it is *significant*. The reasons for this are:

- the cost in staff time and money outweighs any potential savings
- it is demotivating to highlight minor differences; staff feel that management is being petty
- being aware of a minor variance does not help the decision-making process; the variance is too small to draw any conclusions from

This approach to reporting variance is known as **exception reporting**. Exception reporting should be the normal approach adopted by a well-run company.

Fixed and flexible budgets

To monitor performance adequately, **flexible budgets** are needed. An example of a flexible budget will make this clear:

Mohammed Iqbal is a materials purchasing manager. His budgeted spending for the month was £500. Budgeted production for the month was 250 units. Actual production was 300 units, and Mr Iqbal spent £570 on raw materials. Has Mr Iqbal done well or badly?

Using a **fixed** budget for comparison:

Budgeted spending	Actual spending	Variance
£500	£570	£70 (adverse)

However, more units than expected were produced. If Mr Iqbal was allowed £500 to buy raw materials for 250 units, this works out at £2 raw material **per unit**.

Therefore, using a **flexible** budget:

Flexible budget spending	Actual spending	Variance
(300 units × £2)= £600	£570	£30 (favourable)

The flexible budget gives a truer picture of how Mr Iqbal has done. The flexible budget takes into account **different levels of production**.

Behavioural aspects of budgets

When looking at the procedure for preparing budgets, much reference was made to involving relevant staff. A good budget system should allow those responsible for *managing* a budget to have some say in setting the budget *level*.

The reason for this is simple – people feel happier achieving their own targets than targets someone else has set for them.

PC 3
PC 4
C 3.1

ACTIVITY

You can run a mile in 4 mins 50 secs at present. Your coach has set you a target of running the mile in 3 mins 45 secs (close to the world record!).

As a group, discuss how you would feel if set such a target. Do you think it would make you work harder?

PC 4

ACTIVITY

Can you think of any examples of unrealistic targets set in your workplace?

By involving people, they feel part of the whole budgeting process, and are much more likely to try and achieve budget targets. If a budget is simply *imposed* on a group of workers, their reaction may be to reject the budget, and make no effort to meet the imposed targets.

Besides encouraging people to achieve budget targets, involving them in the budget process has wider benefits. Senior management asking the opinion of workers and budget holders (including middle management) has the effect of creating a better industrial relations environment. There is less hostility towards management, and less of an 'us and them' attitude.

There are dangers in giving too much freedom to staff to set their own budget, however. A classic example is that of **budget padding**. Here, a budget is set artificially high by a manager. For example, the IT manager in a company wants a budget of £100 000 for new equipment next year.

Because she is competing against other departments for funds, the manager asks for £120 000.

Another example of budget padding is where a budget holder is judged on how adverse the variance from budget is. The budget holder may add a bit extra 'just to be safe'. The budget holder for office stationery may 'pad' the budget to prevent the budget being overspent.

Neither example above encourages efficiency!

A possible way of avoiding budget padding is to use zero-based budgeting.

■ Using budgets to evaluate managers

Where the manager is a budget holder, budget variance can be used as a means of assessing the manager's performance. There are two main strategies a company can adopt:

1. Regard keeping to a budget as the most important part of a manager's job.
2. Tolerate adverse budget variances, by looking at the long-term benefits to the company of the manager's work.

PC 4
C 3.1

ACTIVITY

Which approach do you think is best? As a group, discuss how you might react if faced with either strategy.

The danger of adopting the first approach is that managers *only* concentrate on keeping to budget. In reality, managing a budget is only one part of a manager's role. If he becomes obsessed with keeping within a budget, he may ignore other areas of his job. He may upset other staff who work for him, causing staff to leave or go off sick.

The second approach gives a broader assessment of a manager's role. It says that managers need to be judged against many different criteria, not just against a single budget figure. The increased flexibility offered by this approach can be illustrated by this example:

Elise Hunter is a departmental sales manager in a clothing company. Her department makes football jerseys. She has control of an advertising budget. During the year, England win the world cup. Should she:

1. advertise the England football jerseys and sell many more, even though this will exceed her advertising budget, or
2. keep to her existing advertising budget?

The common sense answer is to increase the advertising. This will help the company achieve its goal of increased profit, and Elise will be doing her job better. Under the first, narrower, budgetary approach to evaluating staff performance, Elise would be worried about exceeding her advertising budget.

ACTIVITY

PC 4

Can you think of any example of 'budget obsessiveness' in your workplace or college which has had bad effects on the people who work there?

Studies have shown that adopting the narrower approach often results in greater anxiety, leading to higher sickness levels and staff turnover.

■ Tight vs. loose budgets

PC 3

A loose budget is one that allows staff to adopt a lazy approach and yet still achieve budget targets. Obviously, such a budget does little to motivate staff or encourage efficiency.

A tight budget, on the other hand, may be very difficult to achieve, resulting in staff giving up any attempt to meet it!

What is needed is something in between. The ideal budget is one that is set *just a bit tighter* than what the staff themselves feel they can achieve. This has the effect of motivating them to achieve the little bit extra needed to meet the target. Finding exactly the right level at which to set the budget requires a good deal of skill, not to say luck!

What makes a good budget system?

From what has been said about budgets, the following key features of a good budget system can be identified:

1. There must be a plan, expressed in numbers or money. It must be possible to compare the plan with what actually happens in the business.
2. Comparison between the plan and the actual performance needs to take place. It is important that the same aspect is measured in both plan and actual performance. For instance, labour efficiency must be calculated in the same way for both plan and actual performance.
3. The comparison must be made frequently; this is the *monitoring* part of the budget system.
4. Where variances occur, it is essential that the person responsible is informed. Otherwise, an adverse variance can't be corrected. The quicker the responsible person is told the better.
5. The budget must be quickly adaptable to changing circumstances. Sudden oil price rises in the 1970s must have thrown many chemical company raw materials budgets out!
6. The budget system needs to be seen by staff in a positive light. If it is regarded simply as a checking system, the results of which are used to criticise staff, people will be resentful of the system. A good budget system encourages staff to contribute towards the company achieving its goals.
7. Finally, the budget system must not cost more time and money to operate than it saves!

SUMMARY

1 Monitoring is essential to draw attention to problems quickly.

2 The difference between budgeted and actual figure is a variance.

3 Variances are adverse when bad for the company, favourable when good.

4 Exception reporting saves time and money, and avoids demotivating staff.

5 A flexible budget takes into account varying levels of output. It is better for comparison purposes than a fixed budget.

6   Budget targets need to be realistic to avoid demotivating staff. Relevant staff need to be involved in the budgeting process.

7   There are dangers in having too tight or loose a budget.

8   Good budget systems are adaptable, involve frequent monitoring, and are regarded positively by staff.

FURTHER ACTIVITY

PC 3
PC 4
C 3.1

Discuss in a group how you would feel in the following circumstances:

(i)   being given an impossible budget target to achieve
(ii) being given a standstill target
(iii) being given an attainable target

Try to relate your discussion to any budget in the workplace a member of the group may have encountered.

QUESTION

PC 1
PC 4
AN 3.2
AN 3.3

Phil Walters works in the photographic department of an advertising agency. He has been called in by his boss who is worried about how much Phil has spent on film.

'You only had a £2000 budget to spend on film, and you've spent £2600,' his boss tells him.

'Ah, but that was for an estimated 50 photocalls, and I've done 70 so far,' Phil replies.

Using a flexible budget, show whether Phil has been using the film efficiently or not.

Element 11.2 Assignment

For a local organisation or college, complete the following tasks:

PC 2
PC 4
C 3.2
AN 3.1
AN 3.3

Task 1
Show in a diagram the budget-setting process for the organisation. Your diagram should show the various stages, mention personnel involved, and types of budget produced.

PC 1
PC 3
C 3.3

Task 2
Prepare a sales budget for the forthcoming budget period. State which factors (e.g. inflation, market growth) you have taken into consideration when setting the budget.

PC 2
PC 3
AN 3.1
AN 3.2
AN 3.3

Task 3
For **one** of the budgets you have mentioned, outline the monitoring process in a memo to a new member of staff.

Element 11.3

IDENTIFY APPROACHES USED IN BUSINESS TO MONITOR THE USE OF FINANCIAL RESOURCES

PERFORMANCE CRITERIA

1 **Methods of classifying cost are evaluated**
   Range: by element, function, nature

2 **Costing systems are compared**
   Range: absorption, marginal, standard and activity-based costing; linkage to stock valuation methods

3 **Procedures for monitoring outcomes are identified**
   Range: variance analysis for labour, load factors, overheads

4 **Role of cost data in pricing decisions is explained**
   Range: cost-plus, market led

EVIDENCE INDICATORS

A case study to identify the most suitable methods of classifying and monitoring reporting systems related to costs for two different types of business.

An analysis of the cost of a product with recommendations on pricing justified.

6 Costing – an introduction

All businesses sell products. These can be goods or services. **Costing** tells the business how much the product costs to produce. Without this information, it might be difficult for the business to know what price to charge for its products, or know where to look for cost-cutting. PC 1

The process of costing products is part of **cost accounting**, and is an important part of any business. Unlike balance sheets and profit and loss accounts, businesses do not have to produce cost accounts by law. Costing is done for **internal** reasons – it is used by management to help them make decisions.

ACTIVITY

Can you think of any reasons why a business would *not* want to publish cost accounts?

Some costing information is **commercially sensitive** – if a business's competitors knew what the costings for a contract were, for example, it would make it easier for the competitor to put in a lower bid and win the contract.

The four main reasons why businesses cost products are:

1. To help set a selling price for the product. Businesses which make a wide range of products often set the selling price by simply adding a mark-up to the cost price of a product, for example:

Cost = £10. Add mark-up of 25%
Selling price = £10 + £2.50
= £12.50

2. To decide whether a particular product is profitable or not. If the selling price is less than the cost, or if the percentage mark-up is too low, the business may decide to stop making that product.

To understand this, look at the following example:

Rogerson PLC make three products.
Total sales = £36 000
Total expenses = £23 000
NET PROFIT = £13 000

Analysis of each product:

Product	A	B	C
Sales	£16 000	£10 000	£10 000
Costs	£7000	£11 000	£5000
Profit	£9000	– £1000	£5000

If Rogerson PLC were to stop making product B, their profit would increase to £14 000. Check these calculations to make sure you agree.

3. To put a value on the stock of goods. This is covered more fully in the chapter on stock valuation.

4. To help management compare the actual cost with budgeted cost. Costing is, therefore, an important part of the budgeting process.

The classification of costs

· The different types of cost can best be illustrated by looking at a particular product made by a firm:

Francome Ltd make wooden boxes. There are several costs that the firm has:

rent and rates £5000/year
heating and lighting £2600/year
raw materials £6.50 per box
wages £100/week for each worker; the workers make 50 boxes a week each

If we want to find the **cost** of making each box, there are several different answers!

Just the cost of materials = £6.50 per box

But as Francome Ltd pay people to make the boxes, a better answer would include this cost:

Cost of box = cost of materials + cost of labour
= £6.50 + (100/50)*
= £6.50 + £2
= £8.50 per box

* (each worker makes 50 boxes a week, and is paid £100, so the labour cost per box is £2)

A third approach would be to include a share of other costs such as rent, rates, heating and so on. After all, there would be no need to rent a factory if Francome weren't making boxes! In fact, one method of costing, known as **absorption costing,** does include such costs, and this will is looked at in another chapter.

Before a product can be costed, you need to know *which* costs are to be included. To do this, the costs need to be *classified*.

Costs can be classified in three ways:

- by behaviour
- by function
- by nature

■ Classification by behaviour

Cost behaviour is defined as **the way in which costs are affected by changes in the level of output.**

Fixed and variable costs

Looking at the above example, the costs can be divided into **fixed** and **variable** costs.

A fixed cost is one that stays the same, no matter how many boxes are produced. A variable cost is one that changes depending on the number of boxes produced.

ACTIVITY

Which are the FIXED and VARIABLE costs in making boxes?

ACTIVITY

Listed below are some of Angelo's pizza restaurant costs. Say whether the following costs are fixed or variable:

food ingredients
rent
rates
gas for cookers
mortgage payment
manager's wages
part-time staff wages

The mortgage payment is a fixed cost, even though the amount paid might change, because it *doesn't* depend on how many meals are served – it still has to be paid!

The manager's wages are fixed because s/he gets paid the same whether the restaurant is busy or not. The part-time staff, on the other hand, are variable costs – more get taken on when the restaurant is busy, less when it is quiet. Any salaried worker is, therefore, a fixed cost.

The difference between fixed and variable costs can be seen in the form of a graph (*see* Fig. 6.1).

Step costs

Certain costs such as rent, rates and salaried workers are classified as fixed costs – costs which do not change with the amount the firm produces. While this may be true for a short time, there are situations when classifying them as fixed costs is inaccurate.

A company might be renting a factory for £5000 a year. After a time, it finds that the factory has become too small – there is no room for any more machinery, and it is impossible to increase output. If the company wants to produce more, it needs to move to a bigger factory, where the rent is £7000 a year.

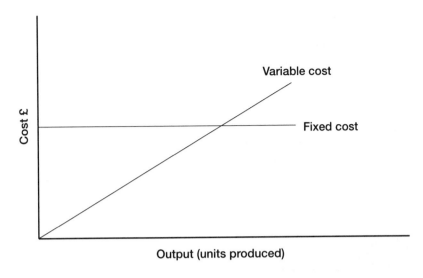

Fig. 6.1   The difference between fixed and variable costs

This new factory might be OK until production reaches a level where no more can be produced. The company has to move again, to premises costing £10 000 a year to rent.

In this case, the rent is a **step** cost (*see* Fig. 6.2).

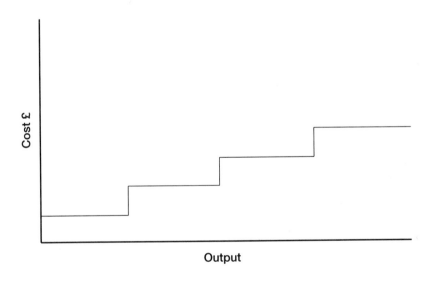

Fig. 6.2   Step costs

Instead of increasing directly with level of output, the rent goes up in *steps*.

Other examples of step costs are salaried workers. If a company needs one sales representative to cover 100 shops, then increasing the number of shops to 101 means an extra sales representative will have to be paid.

Semi-variable costs

These are costs which are part fixed, part variable. A good example is a telephone bill. This consists of a **standing charge** and a **usage charge** (i.e. for each call made).

ACTIVITY

Which charge on the telephone bill is the FIXED part?

The standing charge is *fixed*, whereas the usage charge is *variable*. This means that the total telephone bill goes up with increased usage.

Figure 6.3 illustrates this in graph form.

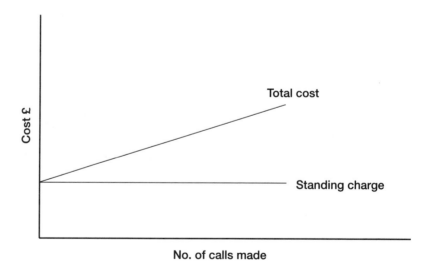

Fig. 6.3 Semi-variable costs

■ Classification by function

This method of classification is a traditional one, and looks at where the costs occur in a business. There are three main categories:

1. production costs
2. administration costs
3. distribution and selling costs

Most expenses that occur can easily be put into one of these categories. Examples of each category are:

1. Production costs
   Raw material costs; shopfloor labour costs; machinery costs; factory rent costs.
2. Administration costs
   Office salaries; general management salaries; accountancy fees; computer systems.
3. Selling and distribution costs
   Transport manager's salary; sales managers' salaries; commission paid; advertising; postage and packing of finished product.

In addition to the three main categories, there can also be :

- research and development costs – these occur when new products are being developed and tested
- finance costs – the costs of borrowing money to run the business (typically loan interest)

ACTIVITY

PC 1

Can you think of any more examples of the three main cost categories?

■ Classification by nature

Unit costs

These are one of the most important costs for a cost accountant. A unit cost is *the total cost* of a *single unit*. The single unit can be a product, or a service such as a haircut. There are several different methods of calculating the cost of a single unit, each of which can give a different answer.

At this stage, this is best summarised for a product as:

	£
Raw materials	12
Labour	5
	17
add: Share of factory overheads (rent, etc.)	6
	23
add: Share of admin overheads (office salaries, office rent, etc.)	4
	27

Notice that in this example, there are *three* different values for **unit cost**. Which figure is used depends on the costing method being employed. The different costing methods will be examined in more detail in the later chapters.

Non-linear costs

Accountants are sometimes criticised for assuming that costs increase in a **linear** fashion. A linear cost will rise in direct proportion to output (*see* Fig. 6.4).

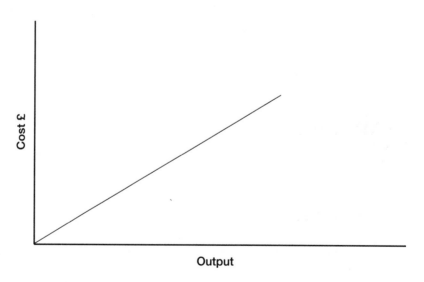

Fig. 6.4 Linear costs

Economists argue, however, that this is a short-term view of cost behaviour. Over the longer term, costs are **non-linear** (*see* Fig. 6.5).

In Fig. 6.5, the line shows **economies of scale**. Here, costs do not rise *as much* as output. Economies of scale occur where greater production leads to savings.

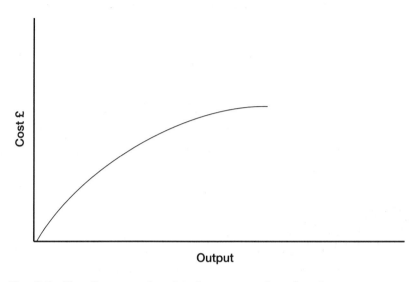

Fig. 6.5 Non-linear costs, showing economies of scale

A good example is in the purchase of raw materials. The bigger the purchase, the more discount a buyer can expect. The **unit cost** of the raw materials decreases as more is bought.

Other examples of economies of scale include:

- production lines (where less labour is needed to produce a single item)
- a sales team selling many different products (cheaper per product than having the team selling just a few products)

The opposite situation also occurs. In Fig. 6.6, costs rise proportionally *more* than output. Such cases are known as **diseconomies of scale**.

An example is where a machine is overworked by increased production. The machine starts to break down more frequently; repair bills increase at a faster rate than output increases.

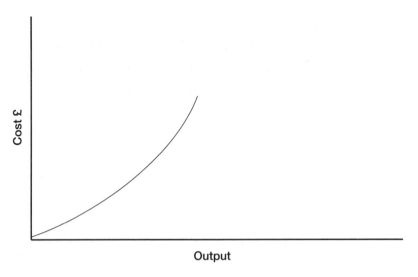

Fig. 6.6 Diseconomies of scale

Sunk cost

Imagine you are selling your house, so decide to paint it. You have a choice between two types of paint:

- an expensive paint costing £10 which will last five years
- a cheaper paint costing £6 which will only last two years

Which paint should you choose?

Common sense says the cheaper paint; after all, hopefully you are moving soon! However, if you already had some expensive paint, there would be no point in buying *more* paint. You would use the expensive paint! No matter how much the paint cost you in the past, it is a cheaper option than buying new paint.

In other words, because the paint has already been bought, it is a cost that is in the past: a **sunk cost**.

The general rule is: **ignore sunk costs** when making a decision. Once a cost has been incurred, it is impossible to 'turn back the clock'.

It is tempting, but foolish, to throw good money after bad. Because a project has cost you a lot of money in the past, you invest more money to finish it, even though this means losing more money.

A famous example is Concorde. It would have been much cheaper to abandon the project than to complete it and have a loss-making aircraft. Unfortunately, not even governments always understand the concept of sunk cost!

Fig. 6.7   Concorde *(photograph by Adrian Meredith, Adrian Meredith photography)*

ACTIVITY

See if you can find any other examples of expensive projects where large sunk costs have led to the completion of a loss-making product.

PC 1

Opportunity cost

This is a notion that accountants have borrowed from economists.

> An opportunity cost can be defined as: **the cost of not doing something else with a resource**.

To understand this, look at this example:

A large company has a factory producing component Z. The factory makes a profit each year. The managing director believes the factory space could be rented out for £9000 a year.

£9000 is the **opportunity cost** of *not* renting the factory out. That is to say: we *could* have £9000 *if* we rented the factory out.

ACTIVITY

What would you need to know before deciding whether to rent the factory space out to someone else?

SUMMARY

1 Costing is an internal activity, done to aid decision making.

2 There are three main ways of classifying costs: by behaviour; by function; by nature.

3 Cost behaviour includes fixed and variable costs. It looks at the way the cost changes with level of output.

4 Some costs are neither truly fixed nor variable. These can be step costs or semi-variable costs.

5 Functional costs are classified by where they occur in the business.

6 Costs classified by nature include: non-linear costs; sunk costs; opportunity costs.

7 There are several different ways of calculating unit cost.

Classify the following costs by function:

- Sales staff car expenses
- Machinery repair
- Transport fleet repair
- Factory rent
- Office rent
- Managing director's salary
- Foreman's salary

7 Absorption costing

PC 2

Absorption costing is one of the main methods of cost accounting. Businesses incur costs which cannot be attributed to a particular product. Examples of such costs are:

- rent
- rates
- salaries of office staff

Such costs are known as **overheads**. In a manufacturing industry, overheads can be much bigger than costs such as raw materials.

Absorption costing is **a method of sharing the cost of the overheads between products.**

PC 1

Direct and indirect costs

In classifying costs, a distinction was made between **fixed** and **variable** costs. For absorption costing, a different classification needs to be used. In this new classification, costs are either **direct** or **indirect**.

A **direct cost** is one that is attributable only to a specific product.

An **indirect cost** is one that occurs in the business, but *can't* be attributed to a specific product.

Examples of **direct** costs are:

- raw materials
- 'piece rate' wages paid to workers
- commission paid to someone for selling a particular product

Examples of **indirect** costs include:

- factory rent (where the factory makes more than one product)
- office staff wages
- interest paid on bank loans
- staff canteen

How does this compare with fixed and variable costs?

Students often make the mistake of thinking that direct costs are the same as variable costs, and indirect costs the same as fixed costs. This is not always the case.

For example, consider the electricity used to run a machine. If this is metered, you can tell exactly how much it has cost you. Also, the amount of electricity used *varies directly* with the amount the machine produces (i.e. output).

The electricity cost is therefore a **variable cost**.

But, if more than one product is made on the machine, it is impossible to attribute the cost to a *single product*. Therefore, it is an **indirect cost**.

Alternatively, depreciation of a piece of equipment used solely to make a single product is a **direct** cost. If the depreciation does not change with *how many* units of the product are made, then it is a **fixed cost**.

ACTIVITY

State whether these are direct or indirect costs:

- foreman's wages (who oversees the production of a single product)
- depreciation of office equipment
- depreciation of delivery van
- depreciation of machine (used in the construction of a single product)
- personnel manager's salary
- factory heating
- electricity

What are overheads?

Overheads are quite simply **indirect costs**. Anything that isn't a **direct cost** is therefore an overhead.

> The total of direct costs, such as direct raw materials and direct labour, is known as **prime cost**.

■ Types of overhead

If we recall the previous chapter, we saw that costs can be classified by **function**. When overheads are classified this way, they are split into:

- production overheads
- administrative overheads
- distribution and selling overheads

Absorption costing – the three stages

We have said that the basic idea of absorption costing is to share *all overheads* (indirect costs) between the products. In other words, all the overhead cost was 'added on' to the *direct* cost of the product.

We shall now look at how the overhead costs are shared.

Three stages are involved in applying absorption costing:

Stage 1 *Allocating* the cost to a particular cost centre.

Stage 2 *Apportioning* overhead costs between the various departments.

Stage 3 *Absorption* of the department costs to unit costs.

These stages can be remembered as the 'three As' – Allocation, Apportionment and Absorption.

■ Allocation

All overhead (i.e. indirect) costs are *allocated* (i.e. given) to a particular **cost centre**. These cost centres can be:

- production departments

- service departments (e.g. a department which repairs machinery in all the production departments, or a stores department)
- administrative departments (e.g. wages office, secretarial department)
- sales and distribution departments (e.g. packaging department, sales office)
- other cost centres (these might be items such as rent, rates, insurance which are shared across all departments).

■ Apportionment

In this stage, the aim is to divide up all the overhead costs connected with production and send them (allocate) to particular **production departments**.

(Some of the overhead costs can be attributed directly to a particular production department, without dividing up, such as machinery depreciation.)

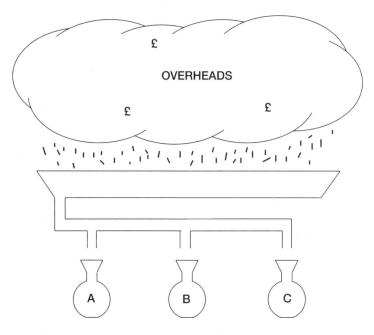

Fig. 7.1 Under absorption costing, overheads are apportioned between units of production

■ Absorption

The final stage involves production department overheads being **added to** the direct costs of producing units.

Which overheads are included?

A share of overheads is added to the direct unit cost in absorption costing:

Unit cost of product X

	£
	£
Direct materials and labour (prime cost)	4.00
Share of production overhead	2.50
	6.50
Share of administration overhead	1.30
	7.80
Share of selling + distribn overhead	2.25
	10.05

There are three possible values for unit cost. The most commonly used is:

> **unit cost = direct costs + share of production overhead**

The unit cost obtained this way is sometimes referred to as **factory cost**. This method is also used for **stock valuation** purposes.

Sometimes the full share of administration overheads and selling and distribution overheads are also included. This gives a **cost of sales** figure, rather than factory cost.

PC 2
AN 3.1
AN 3.2

ACTIVITY

If ten units of the above product are produced and sold, what is the:

(i) total factory cost
(ii) cost of sales
(iii) prime cost?

As production overheads are usually the only costs apportioned, we will only consider these from here onwards.

It is worth reminding ourselves exactly what the term 'production overhead' includes. This can include costs such as rent or rates. Rent for the whole factory pays for production department, administration department and sales departments. In this case, *some* of the rent will be 'sent' to the production department during apportionment.

Service departments, which repair machinery in several production departments, are also regarded as **production overheads**.

A staff canteen which services production staff can also be regarded as a production overhead.

Once the overheads have been shared out (apportioned), absorption may seem an easy matter. In practice, though, it is quite complicated, and is dealt with more fully in the next chapter.

Apportionment – further considerations

In apportionment, a production overhead is shared between various products (or departments). Absorption costing aims to divide *all* overheads between individual products. How the overheads are divided up is very important – if overheads are not shared realistically, the absorption costing is of little use.

A simple example will demonstrate this:

A woodworking factory makes three products: chairs, coffee tables and sideboards.

Renting the factory costs £6500 a year.

The following information is available:

	Chairs	Coffee tables	Sideboards
No of units sold	100	80	30
Sales value (£)	1000	1850	3300
Floor area occupied (sq. m)	325	130	195

Under the absorption costing system, the £6500 rent needs to be **apportioned** and allocated to each product. How should this be done?

■ Basis of apportionment

An obvious answer is to divide the rent equally between the three products. However, as can be seen from the sales figures, this would not be very fair.

What we need to ask is: how much of the rent cost is each product 'responsible' for? From the figures above, it is clear that chairs take up more factory floor space than the other products, so chairs should bear a greater share of the rent cost.

Floor area is used as the **basis of apportionment**; the cost of the rent is split between the products in the same proportion as the floor area used.

In the above example, this would result in each product receiving the following share of rent:

Factory rent = £6500 a year

	Chairs	Coffee tables	Sideboards	TOTAL
Floor area occupied (sq. m)	325	130	195	650
Share of rent:	$\frac{325}{650} \times 6500$	$\frac{130}{650} \times 6500$	$\frac{195}{650} \times 6500$	
	= £3250	= £1300	= £1950	£6500

There are several commonly used bases of apportionment in absorption costing. Try the activity on page 71 (answers are at the end of the chapter):

ACTIVITY

Match the following overheads with the most suitable basis of apportionment:

Overhead	*Basis of apportionment*
Rates	a) Number of employees per department
Rent	b) Floor area
Machine maintenance costs	c) Volume of space occupied
Staff canteen	d) Machine book value
Depreciation of equipment	e) No. of machine hours worked
Heating	
Lighting	
Personnel department wages	
Building repairs	

Notice that there is more than one basis of apportionment for certain overheads, such as heating. The answer shown first is the more commonly used basis of apportionment. (For heating, this is volume.)

Now try the question at the end of the chapter.

Service departments

These include the maintenance department and factory canteen. To recap, both are part of **production** and therefore are production overheads. What needs to be done is to apportion these overheads to production departments. From there the costs can be **allocated** to units.

In Fig. 7.2, the overheads associated with service departments A and B are apportioned and allocated to the three production departments. A complication arises, however, when we consider an overhead such as rent.

The rent is initially apportioned between the *five* departments (i.e. the two service departments and three production departments). The share of overhead thus added to the service departments needs to be **re-apportioned** and allocated to the three production departments.

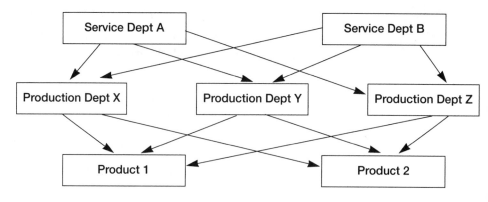

Fig. 7.2 Apportionment and allocation

This is an example of re-apportionment:

Silverwell Ltd have a maintenance department to service their three production departments. The following figures are available:

	£
Maintenance overheads	5 400
Canteen costs	3 000
Rent	8 400
	16 800

	Dept A	Dept B	Dept C	Mainten.	TOTAL
Floor area (sq.m)	80	100	40	20	240
Machine hours	200	250	150	–	600
No. of employees	12	18	9	6	45

Below is how you would apportion the overheads between the three production departments:

	Dept A	Dept B	Dept C	Mainten.	TOTAL
	£	£	£	£	£
Rent	2800	3500	1400	700	8 400
Canteen costs	800	1200	600	400	3 000
Maint. o/heads	1800	2250	1350	–	5 400
	5400	6950	3350	1100	16 800

(Check to see how we have arrived at these figures.)

The maintenance department overheads now need to be **re-apportioned** between the three production departments. Machine hours will be used as the basis of re-apportionment:

	Dept A £	Dept B £	Dept C £	TOTAL
Share of Maintenance dept overheads:	$\frac{200}{600} \times 1100$ = £367	$\frac{250}{600} \times 1100$ = £458	$\frac{150}{600} \times 1100$ = £275	£1100

Add to existing share of overheads:

	Dept A £	Dept B £	Dept C £	TOTAL £
	5400	6950	3350	
	367	458	275	
	5767	7408	3625	16 800

SUMMARY

1 Absorption costing shares overheads between products.

2 Direct costs are attributable to a specific product; indirect costs are not.

3 The total of direct costs is known as prime cost.

4 Overheads are classified by function into: production; administrative; distribution and selling.

5 The three stages of absorption costing are: Allocation; Apportionment; Absorption.

6 A basis of apportionment gives a means of dividing overhead between products or departments.

7 Sometimes, overheads need to be re-apportioned to production departments.

QUESTION

Fulcrum Ltd have the following overhead costs:

	£
Building repairs	2000
Rent	16 000
Rates	4000
Heating	6000
Lighting	1800
Canteen	720
Maintenance	4000
Machine depreciation	2400

Information relating to the four departments is as follows:

Department	A	B	C	D
Floor space (sq.m)	240	160	320	80
Volume (cubic m)	600	280	1200	320
No. of employees	18	9	12	21
Machine hours worked	2000	3000	3000	4000
Book value of machines	2400	800	1600	1600

Show how the various overheads will be apportioned between the four departments.

Answer to task on page 71

Rates	b)
Rent	b)
Machine maintenance costs	e) or d)
Staff canteen	a)
Depreciation of equipment	d)
Heating	c) or b)
Lighting	c) or b)
Personnel Dept wages	a)
Building repairs	b)

8 Absorption of overheads

The final stage of absorption costing is where the share of overheads is **absorbed**, or added to, the individual product.

PC 2

Remember that only **production overheads** are added to the cost of production; administration, selling and distribution overheads are simply added to cost of sales, and do not form part of the **unit cost** of a particular product.

A difficulty with overhead absorption

As mentioned in the previous chapter, overhead absorption is not as simple as it may appear. To understand why, consider the following situation:

A company makes and sells products throughout the year. It does not know the exact cost of certain overheads, such as heating and electricity, until the end of the year, when the final quarter bill arrives.

If the company does not know how much the overheads are, how can they be apportioned and absorbed onto a product? Without absorbing overhead into unit cost, absorption costing is useless: how can unit cost be known, and selling price determined?

Obviously the company cannot wait until the end of the year before working out unit cost (and hence selling price). No customer will buy a product unless they know what the price is!

■ Pre-determined absorption rates

The solution to this problem is to use a **pre-determined absorption rate**.

Instead of waiting until the overhead costs are known exactly, the overheads are *estimated*. The **activity level** is also estimated at the start of the year.

Dividing estimated overhead by estimated activity level gives the overhead absorption rate:

Estimated overheads £12 000
Estimated production (units) 500

Absorption rate = £24 per unit

Note that 'estimated' figures are **budget** figures, and are derived from the budgeting process. Why can't actual overhead costs be calculated more frequently?

It would be possible to measure overheads more frequently than once a year – once a month, for instance. The problem with then using these overhead figures as a basis for pricing is that the overheads vary throughout the year.

For example, factory heating overhead is likely to be highest during the winter months. If a higher amount of overhead was then absorbed onto a product, the product's price would rise in winter! Clearly, this is not a very satisfactory way of dealing with overheads.

Activity level

The estimated activity level for the year can be expressed in several ways:

- the number of units produced
- the total machine hours worked
- the total labour hours worked
- the level of direct costs

As there are several different measures of activity level, we can therefore calculate several *different* absorption rates.

For example:

The budgeted production overheads and other costs for Waltham Manufacturing Ltd production department Z are as follows:

Budgeted	£
Overheads	45 000
Machine hours	2000
Labour hours	18 000
Direct materials cost	90 000
Direct labour cost	36 000
No. of units produced	4500

The absorption rates are:

(i)   Per unit produced = $\dfrac{£45\,000}{4500}$ = £10 per unit

(ii) Rate per machine hour = $\dfrac{£45\,000}{2000}$ = £22.50 per machine hr

(iii) Rate per direct labour hour = $\dfrac{£45\,000}{18\,000}$ = £2.50 per dir lab hr

(iv) Percentage of direct material cost = $\dfrac{£45\,000}{£90\,000}$ = 50%

(v)   Percentage of direct labour cost = $\dfrac{£45\,000}{£36\,000}$ = 125%

If this seems confusing, remember that we are selecting a **basis on which to add overheads to a department**.

In the above example, for every machine hour worked, £22.50 of overhead will be 'added' or absorbed onto the department cost. Likewise, for every direct labour hour worked, £2.50 of overhead will be 'added' to the department cost. With bases (iv) and (v), for every £1 spent on the direct cost, a percentage of that amount is 'added' to the department cost.

Try the activity below to see if you have grasped this concept, and then check with the answer at the end of the chapter.

ACTIVITY

If actual spending on direct materials was £80 000, how much overhead would be absorbed? (*See* page 83 for the answer.)

PC 2
AN 3.2

Notice that a different answer results from choosing a different basis for absorption rate. If all the **actual** figures had been the same as the **budgeted** figures, it would not have mattered which basis for absorption rate we chose; the same (i.e. budgeted) amount of overhead would have been absorbed.

In practice, it is very unlikely that budgeted and actual figures are the same. Therefore, the cost accountant needs to decide *which* absorption rate to use. There is no definite answer to this; it depends on the nature of the business. In a business where machinery is a major cost, a predetermined absorption rate based on machine hours worked would be best.

Alternatively, in a business where the raw material costs were significant, an absorption rate based on a percentage of raw material costs would be more suitable.

PC 2

ACTIVITY

Which absorption rate would be most suitable for a business which needs a lot of direct labour?

■ Predetermined absorption rate and unit cost

The effect of choosing a different basis for absorption rate can make a lot of difference in the final unit cost figure. Hence this can affect decisions such as whether to continue making the product, what price to charge and so on.

This is best illustrated by going back to our example of Waltham Manufacturing Ltd.

Using the same predetermined absorption rates, let us assume that the company makes a garden lawn trimmer, with these unit costs:

- raw materials – £100
- direct labour cost – £42
- no. of machine hours – 2.1 hrs
- no. of labour hours – 19 hrs

Using the various absorption rates, the overhead absorbed per unit (i.e. a single garden lawn trimmer) is:

(i) per machine hour rate:
     2.1 hrs $\times$ £22.50
     = £47.25

(ii) per direct labour hour rate:
     19 hrs $\times$ £2.50
     = £47.50

(iii) as a percentage of direct raw material cost:
     50% $\times$ £100
     = £50

(iv) as a percentage of direct labour cost:
     125% $\times$ £42
     = £52.50

The point made already about choosing the 'best' basis for absorption rate applies to units as well as departments; it is of great importance in the decision-making process.

From production department to unit

So far we have considered the process of absorption costing as far as allocating, apportioning and absorbing overheads to production departments.

As stated in the introduction to absorption costing, the aim is to absorb the overheads to **product units**. This is achieved in exactly the same way as overheads are absorbed to production departments.

A simple example will illustrate this:

Production Department P makes two products: Biffs and Baffs. Budgeted overheads for department P (including share of absorbed overheads) are £4000 a year.

The following budgeted information is available for the two products:

	Biff	Baff
No. of units produced	300	100
Machine hrs per unit	2	4
Direct raw materials/unit	£5	£4
Direct labour/unit	£4	£6
Direct labour hrs/unit	2	3

How do we share the £4000 overhead between the two products?

There are a number of possibilities:

1. equally between the two products
2. in proportion to the no. of machine hours used
3. in proportion to the no. of labour hours used

ACTIVITY

Can you think of any more ways to share the overheads?

Production Department P relies on using expensive machinery, so the cost accountant has decided to apportion overhead on the basis of machine hours used:

Biff   2 machine hrs per unit × 300 units produced
          = 600 machine hours used

Baff   4 machine hours per unit × 100 units produced
          = 400 machine hours used

Total machine hours = 600 + 400
                      = 1000

Share of overheads: *Biff*   *Baff*

$\dfrac{600}{1000}$ × 4000 = £2400 $\dfrac{400}{1000}$ × 4000 = £1600

Notice that the calculation above is a simple way of using rate per machine hour as a predetermined absorption rate:

Rate per machine hour = $\dfrac{£4000}{1000}$ = £4 per machine hour

For Biff, share of overhead = £4 × 2 hrs × 300 units
                              = £2400

For Baff, share of overhead = £4 × 4 hrs × 100 units
                              = £1600

ACTIVITY

Calculate the share of overhead for each product if a rate per labour hour was used as an absorption rate instead.

■ Products made in several departments

Where a product passes through more than one production department, the share of overheads from *each* production department is added to the unit cost:

Product H (cost per unit)	£
Direct materials	4.00
Direct labour	3.00
Prime cost	7.00
Production overhead	
Dept A	1.50
Dept B	2.20
Full cost	10.70

■ Capacity

The activity level can be based on three different types of capacity:

1 Full capacity
This represents the 'ideal' capacity, where there are no losses due to machine breakdown, absenteeism or shortfall in orders.

2 Practical capacity
This is the same as full capacity, minus an estimated allowance for production losses caused by factors such as machine breakdown. As such, it is a more realistic capacity level than full capacity.

3 Budgeted capacity
This is the capacity which results from other budgets, such as sales budget, expected workforce efficiency, workforce availability, and machine reliability.

ACTIVITY

Can you see the similarities between the three types of capacity and the different types of budgeted standard?

SUMMARY

1 **Overheads are often not known until after the product has been made and sold.**

2 **Predetermined absorption rates add a budgeted share of overhead to each unit.**

3 **Activity level can be expressed in terms of: units produced; machine hours worked; total labour hours worked; the level of direct costs.**

4 **Selecting the most suitable absorption rate depends on the nature of the business.**

5 **For products made in more than one department, a share of overhead is added for each department to the unit cost.**

6 **The three levels of capacity are: full; practical; budgeted.**

QUESTION

The budgeted figures for Westhope Construction Ltd are:

Budgeted		£
Overheads		13 500
No. of units produced		27 000
Direct materials (cost)		54 000
Direct materials (kg)	1080	
Machine hours worked	3000	
Labour hours worked	2700	
Labour rate (per hour)		4

(i) Calculate as many different overhead absorption rates as you can from the above figures.

(ii) If actual direct material used was 1200 kg, calculate the overhead absorbed.

Answer to task on page 77

Overhead absorbed = 50% of direct material cost
$\qquad\qquad\qquad$ = 50% of £80 000
$\qquad\qquad\qquad$ = £40 000

QUESTION

Now calculate the five different absorption rates for Jones Engineering Ltd:

Jones Engineering Ltd Production Dept B

(i) Budgeted spending: £

	£
Overheads	12 000
Direct materials	8000
Direct labour	4000
Machine hours worked	2000
Direct labour hours worked	16 000
No. of units produced	4800

(ii) Actual figures: £

	£
Direct materials	9000
Direct labour	4200
Machine hours worked	1800
Direct labour hours worked	20 000
No. of units produced	4400

Calculate the **actual** amount of overhead absorbed using the absorption rates you obtained in your answer to part (i).

9 Over- and under-absorption of overheads

PC 2

Absorption costing, being based on budgeted estimates, inevitably leads to discrepancies between **actual** and **budgeted** absorption figures. For example:

A firm budgeted for:

Overheads	£3000
No. of units produced	600
Overhead absorbed per unit	£5 (based on the two budgeted figures above)

Actual results were:

Overheads	£3400
No. of units produced	700
Overhead incurred (actual)	£3400
Overhead absorbed (700 × £5)	£3500
Over-absorption of overheads	100

Notice that 'budgeted overhead' and 'overhead absorbed' are not the same thing. The **overhead absorption rate**, which determines how much overhead is 'added to' unit cost, was already set at £5 per unit.

Because the absorbed overhead of £3500 is greater than the **actual** overhead, there is an **over-absorption**.

If absorbed overhead is *less than* actual overhead, there is an **under-absorption**.

ACTIVITY

Work out whether there has been an under- or over-absorption in the following situation, and if so, how much.

(*Hint:* you need to calculate the overhead absorption rate first.)

Budgeted overhead: £6000
Budgeted labour hours: 1200

Actual overhead: £5400
Actual labour hours: 1120

ACTIVITY

What would the effect of:
(i) over-absorbing overheads
(ii) under-absorbing overheads
on profit shown at the end of the year?

To find the answer to the above task, let us see the effect on the final accounts. Remember that the more overhead is added, the higher the unit cost. Therefore, if overheads are *over*-absorbed, the unit cost will be shown as *higher* than actual.

In this example, let us assume that there has been £3000 over-absorption of overhead.

Looking at the trading and profit and loss account:

	With over-absorption	Without over-absorption
Sales	100 000	100 000
Cost of sales	70 000	67 000
Gross profit	30 000	33 000
less expenses	12 000	12 000
Net profit	18 000	21 000

Notice that the 'cost of sales' figure is different. By over-absorbing overhead, we mistakenly said that unit costs were higher than they actually were. Subtracting the over-absorbed overhead from cost of sales increases the profit figure.

Therefore, over-absorption of overhead (before adjusting) *understates* the profit figure.

Similarly, under-absorption of overhead *overstates* the profit figure.

(Higher unit costs also mean a higher closing stock. This will affect the stated profit by making it appear higher. This is usually minor compared to the effect on cost of sales, however.)

Reasons for over- and under-absorption

Look at the following table for a typical manufacturing company:

Department	Absorbed o/hd	Actual o/hd	Over/under- absorption
	£	£	£
Processing	15 000	14 200	800
Welding	38 000	39 900	(1900)

There are several possible explanations for the over-absorption in the processing department:

(i)   actual overheads were less than budgeted.
(ii) more units were produced than expected. If overhead is absorbed using units produced as an absorption base, more overhead will be absorbed.
(iii) more machine hours worked. As in (ii), if machine hours is used as the absorption base, the more hours worked, the more overhead absorbed.
(iv) more direct labour hours worked. As for (ii) and (iii), using direct labour hours as an absorption base.

For the welding department, the same reasons can apply in reverse:

(i)   actual overheads higher than budgeted
(ii) fewer units than expected were produced
(iii) fewer machine hours worked
(iv) fewer direct labour hours worked

Whether overheads are under- or over-absorbed depends on *which absorption base* we are using. They are all linked to the level of activity, however.

This illustrates the importance of activity level in absorption costing; the greater the difference between budgeted and actual activity level, the greater the over- or under-absorption of overheads.

The reason for discrepancies between budgeted and actual figures is looked at in more detail in the chapter on variance analysis.

■ Why not use actual overhead costs?

To avoid all the complications of over- or under-absorption, it might seem easier to use actual overhead costs.

To remind ourselves why, these are the main problems with using actual costs:

(i) Costs aren't known in advance, but a selling price still needs to be set.
(ii) If actual costs are measured, say, every month, the product unit cost will vary over the year.

SUMMARY

1 Overheads can be under- or over-absorbed when actual figures differ from budgeted ones.

2 Over-absorption understates profit; under-absorption overstates profit.

3 Over-absorption gives a higher closing stock valuation.

4 Over- or under-absorption is linked to activity level.

5 Actual costs are not used because they are not known in advance, and can vary throughout the year.

PC 2
AN 3.2

1   For department A:

Budgeted overhead   £7000
Budgeted labour hours   140

If actual labour hours worked are
(i)   138
(ii) 155
calculate how much the over- or under-absorption of overhead is for department A in each case (assuming actual overhead is the same as budgeted overhead).

PC 2
AN 3.2
C 3.2

2   Honeybunch Ltd has recently introduced new technology, designed to speed up the production process. Actual overhead for the year was higher than budgeted. However, using a labour hour absorption rate, there was an under-absorption of overhead. You have been asked to write a brief note to the shopfloor manager, explaining how this situation could arise.

10 Marginal costing

Marginal costing adopts a different approach to that used in absorption costing. As we have seen, absorption costing tries to attribute all costs that arise, whether direct or indirect, to a particular product. It does this by adding on a share of overheads. Marginal costing only concerns itself with the **extra cost** of producing more of a product. The extra cost, or **marginal cost** of a product is defined as the 'the extra cost incurred by producing one more unit'. The difference between the two approaches is an important one, and affects the usefulness of information obtained. To understand this, a simple example using both approaches is given below.

Fenders Ltd make car bumpers. The costs per bumper are:

	£
Direct materials	10
Direct labour	8
Share of fixed overheads	3

Fenders Ltd are approached by a firm wanting a bulk purchase of 500 bumpers, for which they are prepared to pay £10 000 (i.e. £20 per bumper). Should Fenders Ltd accept the order?

Using conventional absorption costing, the cost per bumper is

£10 + £8 + £3 (share of o/heads) = £21

For 500 bumpers the cost will be 500 × 21 = £10,500

As the purchase price is £10 000, Fenders Ltd make a 'loss' of £500.

Let's look at the same order, but this time using marginal costing to help us decide whether to accept or not.

Fenders Ltd want to know two things:

- how much do we get from selling the bumpers? (The agreed price of £10 000.)
- how much will it cost to make the bumpers?

Using marginal costing, the answer is:

For a single bumper
  £10 + £8 = £18

For making 500 bumpers, the extra cost is
  500 × £18 = £9000

This is less than the £10 000 Fenders Ltd are paid. The company makes an extra profit of:
  £10 000 – £9000 = £1000
if it accepts the order.

Notice that the marginal costing method *ignores* overheads. Why? Because making 500 more bumpers will *not increase* the overheads. The only extra costs are direct materials and direct labour. (We are assuming that Fenders Ltd haven't had to buy new machinery, etc. to meet the order.)

If Fenders Ltd had only relied on the absorption costing method, they would have rejected the order, and lost the opportunity to earn an extra £1000.

Contribution

Contribution is an important concept in marginal costing. It is defined as the **sales value less variable cost of sales**.

> **Contribution per unit = selling price – variable cost per unit**

Example:

Ace computer keyboard	£
Raw materials per unit	4
Direct labour per unit	12
Variable production overheads (per unit)	7
Variable cost per unit	23
Selling price	35
Contribution per unit	**£12**

Whenever the selling price is *greater than* the variable cost per unit, there is a **positive contribution**.

Contribution is not the same as 'profit'. A business will only make a profit when it has covered its fixed costs. Each unit sold **contributes** an amount towards covering these costs – sell enough units and the business will start to make a profit.

For this reason, contribution is sometimes called **contribution to fixed cost**.

A marginal cost statement

Product:	A	B	C
	£	£	£
Sales	5000	1300	4500
Variable production cost	3600	1200	3000
Contribution	1400	100	1500
			3000
less: fixed costs			1400
PROFIT			1600

The marginal cost statement takes fixed costs into account when calculating profit. However, unlike absorption costing, the fixed costs are dealt with *after* each individual product contribution has been calculated. Absorption costing adds a share of the fixed cost (overhead) on to the **individual product cost**:

Absorption cost statement

Product:	A	B	C
	£	£	£
Sales	5000	1300	4500
Direct production cost	3600	1200	3000
Share of overhead	700	300	400
Profit /(loss)	700	(200)	1100
PROFIT			1600

Variable cost and marginal cost

Generally speaking, the two costs are the same: the extra cost of making one more unit is simply the cost of raw materials, direct labour and any other variable cost (such as royalty payment or variable overhead).

In some circumstances, there can be a big difference between the two. Imagine this situation: It costs £70 to hire a mini-bus, seating 17 passengers. Each passenger increases the fuel bill on a journey by £3.20.

What is the marginal cost of taking an extra passenger?

The answer may seem obvious: the extra £3.20 fuel cost (i.e. the **variable cost**). However, what if that extra passenger is the 18th passenger? The extra, or **marginal** cost, will be £70! A new mini-bus will need to be hired just to take the new passenger!

Therefore, we can say that:

Marginal cost = variable cost + **any increase in fixed costs caused**

Uses of marginal costing

After the example of Fenders Ltd, you may be left wondering why anyone bothers to use absorption costing! Consider this situation:

If Ace Computers Ltd have fixed costs annually of £15 000, what price should they charge for their keyboards if they sell 1000 a year?

Referring to the previous figures:

Ace computer keyboard £

Variable cost per unit 23

Selling price 35

Contribution per unit £12

Total contribution = (£12 × 1000) = £12 000
Fixed costs = £15 000
LOSS = (£3000)

Although each **unit** makes a positive contribution, we still do not make a profit, as the selling price is too low. What is needed is to take into account **fixed costs** (overheads) when deciding price; we need to use **absorption costing**.

Marginal costing is most useful for 'one-off' orders, like the example of Fenders Ltd.

A well-known instance of the use of marginal costing occurs in selling airline tickets. The 'standard fare' charged is calculated by including a share of overheads, such as fuel, landing fees, wages and aircraft depreciation. On a flight to New York, the standard fare can be nearly £1000. However, it is possible to travel on the same flight with a last-minute 'standby' ticket costing less than £100!

Why the difference in price?

If the airline has not sold all the seats at standard fare, it can sell the remaining seats for less, as this will still give a **contribution to fixed costs**.

The variable costs of taking an extra passenger to New York are negligible – one airline meal costing around 50p!

Therefore, whatever the price charged the extra passenger, the airline still makes money. If the passenger pays £100, there is a positive contribution of £99.50.

Fig. 10.1   An aircraft refuelling *(photograph by Adrian Meredith, Adrian Meredith photography)*

ACTIVITY

List examples of where you think marginal costing has been used in setting the price.

Limitations of marginal costing

As has been shown, marginal costing is not appropriate for the normal run of business – by ignoring fixed costs, a firm runs the risk of selling its products too cheaply and making a loss. Absorption costing tackles this problem by giving a share of overheads to the cost of each unit. When using marginal costing to decide whether to accept a one-off order, there are several other points to consider.

1. What will the effect be of selling a product cheaply to one customer? Perhaps other customers will also seek lower prices.

2. By making and selling this particular product, will the firm be missing the chance of producing another, more profitable product? It may be that accepting an order uses machinery which stops other work being done. This is an example of opportunity cost.

3. There are no 'hidden' increases in fixed costs as a result of accepting the order. For example, increasing production to meet the order might result in more breakdowns of the machinery.

■ Marginal vs. absorption costing

At this stage, you may be a little confused as to which method is best. In some cases, a business has little choice. When a Limited Company produces its published (final) accounts, it is recommended by SSAP 9 (*see* Glossary) to use absorption costing for valuing stock and work-in-progress. The choice of method really occurs, therefore, in internal accounting systems, used by management as an aid to decision-making.

To recap, the difference between the two systems lies in their treatment of **fixed costs**.

Absorption costing shares the fixed costs between units of product.

*Marginal costing only includes variable costs when calculating the cost of a unit of product. The fixed costs are matched with **the accounting period in which they occur**, rather than with particular units.*

This is the only difference, but it can have an impact on profit, as the following example illustrates:

A new business has these costs for its first year of operation:

	£
Direct materials	3000
Direct labour	2100
Fixed overheads	1200
Sales	9000

No. of units produced: 300
Stock at end of year: 50 units

The number of units produced, and the fixed overheads, were exactly as budgeted.*

Using absorption costing:

Overhead absorption rate per unit = 1200/300 = £4 per unit

Cost per unit = $\dfrac{(3000 + 2100)}{300}$ + £4 = £21

Profit statement for year:

	£
Sales	9000
less: cost of sales (250 × 21)	5250
Profit	3750

Note: only the share of the overheads absorbed is included in calculating profit. 250 units were sold (300 – 50 remaining stock), each absorbing £4 of fixed overhead.

Using marginal costing:

Marginal cost per unit = $\dfrac{(3000 + 2100)}{300}$ = £17

Profit statement for year:

	£
Sales	9000
less: cost of sales (250 × 17)	4250
	4750
less fixed overheads	1200
Profit	3550

Notice marginal costing shows a lower profit figure because all the overhead has been taken into account. In absorption costing, some of the overhead arising this year has been 'carried over' with the remaining stock to next year.

* This is unlikely, but it makes the calculations in the example simpler.

ACTIVITY

If there is no stock left at the end of next year, will the profit appear higher using absorption or marginal costing?

Which system gives a more consistent result? Under absorption costing, a build-up of stocks (as in the example) shows a higher profit than under marginal costing. If stocks are run down, the opposite holds true. Profits shown by absorption costing *respond to fluctuations in stock levels* more than in marginal costing.

As stock levels *in the long term* tend to keep in line with sales (i.e. firms don't build up stocks year after year), marginal costing reflects this by showing a more even profits distribution over time. An undesirable consequence of absorption costing is that it shows increased profits where a business has increased stocks. Stock build-up is often a sign of trouble – the product is not selling. Absorption costing therefore gives a totally false impression of the business.

Marginal costing is better for deciding whether to accept small 'one-off' orders than absorption costing. By ignoring fixed costs, which would occur anyway. Marginal costing enables managers to see whether an order will give a positive **contribution**.

Absorption costing, on the other hand, can be of more use when planning the selling price of a normal, as opposed to 'one-off' product. With certain items, such as plastic bottles, the variable costs (raw materials and direct labour) are only a small part of the cost of production. Most expense occurs in buying and running the machinery. Absorption costing, by including the major cost of overheads, gives a better idea of what price to charge for the product.

SUMMARY

1 The marginal cost of a product is the cost of producing the extra unit(s).

2 Contribution = selling price – variable cost per unit

3 Contribution is not the same as profit.

4 Marginal costing only considers overheads after the contribution for each individual product has been calculated.

5 Marginal cost = variable cost + any increase in fixed cost.

6 Marginal costing is useful for deciding whether to accept small, one-off orders.

7 Marginal costing cannot be used for stock valuation in published accounts.

8 Marginal costing shows a more even profit figure over time than absorption costing.

ASSIGNMENT

PC 2
PC 4
C 3.1
C 3.2
AN 3.1
AN 3.2
AN 3.3

In a group, make a list of the costs involved in operating a rail line between London and York. (Don't try guessing the amounts!)

How would you go about deciding on a standard ticket price for the journey? Which costing method have you used?

When you have done this, contact British Rail and find out:

a) The standard return fare London–York
b) The price of any cheap-rate fares for the same journey

Explain in a report why there is a difference in price between the two tickets. Refer to marginal and absorption costing in your report, and say which method you think has been used for either ticket, and why.

QUESTIONS

Zwingles Ltd makes children's toys. Monthly production is 1000 units. The selling price per unit is £110. Unit costs are:

- raw materials £14
- direct labour £6
- variable overheads £8

Monthly fixed costs are £32 400

Task 1

Calculate the monthly profit.

PC 2
AN 3.2

Task 2

Zwingles Ltd has the chance to accept two orders; unfortunately there is only enough spare capacity to accept one order.

PC 2
AN 3.2
C 3.2

Order X: 600 units, for which Zwingles Ltd will receive £21 000.

Order Y: 500 units, for which Zwingles Ltd will receive £16 500.

Order X will need further processing, costing an extra £5 per unit; order Y requires no further processing.

Show in a report which order Zwingles Ltd should accept. You should show the monthly profit if order X is accepted, or if order Y is accepted.

Task 3

Write a brief memo to a trainee explaining the potential problems of using marginal costing in this situation.

PC 2
C 3.2

FURTHER ACTIVITY

Bill went to the staff canteen while visiting someone in hospital. He bought a meal for £1.50, and sat down. A diner next to him said, 'You shouldn't be eating here – this is a staff canteen. It's subsidised, so you eating here is costing the hospital money!'

Write a reply which Bill can use, explaining to the other diner why he doesn't agree with him.

11 Standard costing

The two principal costing systems looked at thus far are absorption cost- ing and marginal costing. Standard costing can be used with either system.

> A **standard cost** is an **estimated unit cost.** It is a budgeted, rather than actual cost, and is estimated **before the costs actually occur. Standard costing** is the use of standard costs to help management.

Two typical uses of standard costing are:

- for valuing stocks and production costs. This is covered in more detail in the chapter on Stock Valuation (*see* Chapter 14). It is an alternative to methods such as LIFO and FIFO.
- to help control budgets. Standard costing does this by comparing the budgeted, standard costs (and revenues) with the **actual** costs (and revenues). The resulting difference is known as a **variance**.

Setting standard costs

As standard costs are budgeted, or estimated, figures, it is important that the estimates are as accurate as possible. Standard costs are normally set once a year. As with budgets, it is important that the people setting the standard costs are the right people. Accountants need to work with the managers whose job it is to keep costs down in their department or area.

For example, there is no point setting a standard cost for the price of a raw material if the person who does the buying has not been consulted.

Alternatively, if estimating how efficiently a raw material is being used, the manager of the production department where it is used should be consulted.

> **Standard costing and budgetary control**
> Both use the same idea – setting a target (i.e. budget or standard) against which performance can be measured. Standard costing focuses solely on **production**, whereas budgetary control looks at all aspects of the business. Standard costing is more detailed than budgetary control, and looks closely at human factors, methods of production and operational efficiency.

■ Examples of Standard Costs

1. Standard cost rates

These include:

- Standard wage rate – this is the amount of money that a worker receives for an hour's work.
- Standard raw material cost – the cost per kilo, tonne, etc. of a particular raw material.

2. Performance standards

These include:

- Standard hour – this is the amount of work that (theoretically) gets done in an hour.
- Standard time – this is the time required to produce a single unit, expressed in standard hours. It should include an allowance for any stoppages that are likely to occur, such as sickness or idle time.
- Standard raw material usage – this represents the amount of raw material that should be used to produce a unit of product. As such, it makes an allowance for waste.

An example of standard costing:

Product X

Standard raw material usage	3 kilos
Standard raw material cost	£4 per kilo
Standard time to complete	6 hrs
Standard wage rate	£3.75 per hour

Standard cost per unit:

	£
Raw materials (3 × £4)	12.00
Labour (6 × £3.75)	22.50
Standard cost per unit	34.50

■ The different types of performance standard

Ideal standard

As the name suggests, this represents the best possible situation. For example, it would mean using raw materials as efficiently as possible, and producing as much of the finished product as possible! Obviously, we don't live in a perfect world, so a department is very unlikely to reach the ideal standard.

If workers in the department are given standards to reach that they think are unrealistic, they will either ignore the standards, or worse still, feel demotivated. For these reasons, ideal standards are not widely used.

Attainable standard

Unlike the ideal standard, it is reasonably possible for a department to reach this standard. The attainable standard allows for some wastage and inefficiency, but still assumes that most work is done efficiently.

Attainable standards provide something realistic for the workforce to aim for. As such, they can be useful for motivating staff.

Current standard

This standard is based on the current working conditions. While this might seem the fairest and most realistic, it does not offer any incentive to improve. In a situation where the business faces competition, it needs to improve constantly and attain higher standards.

Basic standard

Even lower than the current standard, the basic standard is one which hasn't changed for a long time, and may be hopelessly out of date. They should be scrapped and new standards put in place. Their only use is as a means of comparing efficiency or performance over a few years.

ACTIVITY

Discuss why setting an ideal standard might not be a good idea.

■ Problems with setting standard costs

These are similar to those associated with setting budgets, and can be summarised as:

- estimating material costs when these change frequently
- estimating efficiency of material usage
- estimating how long it takes someone to make a particular item
- allowing for inflation
- managers feel threatened by the standards, or relax when they have met the standard (rather than striving to improve efficiency, etc.)
- operating a standard cost system may be prohibitively expensive

Standard costs and marginal costing

Standard costs, being budgeted figures, may seem closely related to the absorption costing system. Standard costs can just as easily be used for marginal costing purposes. To understand how, it is important to remember that in either costing system, costs are often not known until after they occur.

When setting a price based on unit cost, for example, a **standard cost** comprising direct labour or direct raw materials may be easier to use than actual cost.

■ The advantages of standard costing

These can be summarised as:

- providing a target against which to assess performance
- allowing variance reporting and exception reporting
- allowing goods to be priced before actual costs are known
- motivating staff to achieve targets (when realistically set)

SUMMARY

1   Standard costing can be used with absorption costing or marginal costing.

2   A standard cost is an estimated unit cost.

3   Standard costing can be used for valuing stocks, and to help control budgets.

4   Standard costing is more focused on production than budgetary control.

5   There are four different types of performance standard: ideal; attainable; current; basic.

6   The problems in setting standard costs are similar to those found in setting budgets.

FURTHER ACTIVITY

PC 2
PC 4
C 3.2

Explain in a memo to a new trainee cost accountant why your firm uses standard costs for calculating the selling price of its products, rather than actual costs.

12 Activity-based costing

PC 2

Activity-based costing is a fairly recent development in cost accounting. One of the drawbacks of traditional absorption costing is that overheads are not absorbed into product costs on a realistic basis.

Activity-based costing addresses the problem by **grouping** costs. The costs are grouped according to what causes them to arise. The cause of the costs arising is known as a **cost driver**. It is the cost driver which is then used as the basis of apportionment.

A simple example will help illustrate this:

Product	X	Y
Quantity produced	200	300
Direct labour hrs/unit	2	3
Machine hours/unit	2	4
No. of orders dealt with	30	15

Overhead costs:	
relating to machines	£60 000
relating to dealing with orders	£18 000
	£78 000

In this example, the overhead costs have been split into two **cost drivers**; the machine activity and dealing with orders.

What this means is the overheads that have arisen are due to those two cost drivers, and it has been estimated that £60 000 of the total £78 000 has arisen due to machine activity.

To see how activity-based costing works when compared to traditional absorption costing, calculate the overheads to be absorbed by products X and Y using:

a) traditional absorption costing, using direct labour hour rate as the basis of apportionment
b) activity-based costing, using the two cost drivers of machine activity and number of orders as bases of apportionment

Answer:

a) using absorption costing:

Product X = 200 units × 2 hrs = 400 hrs
Product Y = 300 units × 3 hrs = 900 hrs
                                   1300 hrs total

Overhead absorption rate = $\dfrac{£78\ 000}{1300}$ (i.e. total o/hds)

= £60/hr

Therefore, Product X absorbs o/hds at 2 × 60 = £120/unit
Product Y absorbs o/hds at 3 × 60 = £180/unit

b) using activity-based costing:

Machine-driven costs = £60 000
Total machine hours = (200 × 2) for X + (300 × 4) for Y
= 1600 hours

Overhead per machine hour = $\dfrac{£60\ 000}{1600}$ = £37.50

Order driven costs = £18 000
Total orders = 30 + 15 = 45

Overhead per order = £400 (i.e. £18 000/45)

So, for Product X:
Total overheads = (400 hrs × £37.50) + (30 orders × £400)
= £27 000

Overhead per unit = $\dfrac{£27\ 000}{200}$ = £135/unit

For Product Y:
Total overheads = (1200 × £37.50) + (15 × £400)
= £51 000

Overhead per unit = $\dfrac{£51\ 000}{300}$ = £170/unit

As can be seen from the results, activity-based costing results in a different, possibly more accurate, apportionment of overheads than normal absorption costing.

SUMMARY

1 Activity-based costing addresses the problem of apportionment basis in absorption costing.

2 Activity-based costing uses the concept of 'cost drivers', activities which result in costs arising.

3 The two methods usually produce a different absorption rate for a product.

FURTHER ACTIVITY

Simkiss Juggling Ltd make three products:

Product	Diablo	Club	Fire stick
Quantity produced	60	120	80
Direct labour hrs/unit ('000s)	4	3	6
Machine hrs/unit	0.8	1.2	0.6
Floor area occupied (m²)	300	450	150

Overhead costs:
relating to labour hours	£21 600
relating to floor area occupied	£9 000
	£30 600

Calculate the overheads to be absorbed by each product using:

(i) An absorption costing approach, with machine hour rate as the basis of apportionment.

(ii) An activity-based costing approach.

13 Variance analysis

Introduction

Using budgets or standard costs as part of a costing system leads to differences between the budgeted and actual performance. The difference is known as a **variance**. The process of measuring and finding reasons for variances is known as **variance analysis**.

■ Adverse and favourable variances

Actual performance can either exceed the budgeted figure, or fall short of it. Take the following two examples:

	Budgeted	Actual	Variance
Direct materials	£6000	£5700	−300
No. of units produced	80	70	−10

In each case, the actual figure is less than the budgeted figure, so the variance is expressed as a **negative** figure.

However, a more useful approach would be to ask: how does the variance affect the business?

Look at each variance separately. Direct materials expenditure is less than expected. This is *good* news, so the variance is **favourable**.

The number of units produced is less than expected, but this is a *bad* result for the business. (Production usually needs to meet budgeted targets, so that enough sales can be made.) In this case, the variance is **adverse**.

■ Labour variances

There are two main factors to consider when analysing labour variances:

- What is the wage rate?
- How efficiently has the work been done?

Consider the following situation:

Budgeted (i.e. standard) wage rate £4 per hour
Standard time to make one unit: 3 hours

The actual results were: 70 units produced, taking 200 hours, at a rate of £4.45 per hour. Analysing the two factors separately, we get:

Labour rate variance

This is the difference between **standard wage rate** and **actual wage rate**, multiplied by the number of hours **actually** worked:

Standard wage rate $= £4$ per hour
Actual wage rate $\quad= £4.45$ per hour

Rate variance $\qquad= (£4 - £4.45) \times 200$
$\qquad\qquad= £(90)$ ADVERSE

Labour efficiency variance

This is the difference between **standard time to produce all units made** and **actual time taken** multiplied by **standard wage rate**:

Standard time $\quad= 3\,\text{hrs} \times 70\,\text{units}$
$\qquad\qquad= 210\,\text{hrs}$
Actual time $\qquad= 200\,\text{hrs}$

Efficiency variance $= (210 - 200) \times £4$
$\qquad\qquad= £40$ FAVOURABLE

Points to note:

(i) To make 70 units, the cost should be: $70 \times £4 \times 3\text{hrs}$

$= £840$

Actual cost $\qquad = £4.45 \times 200$

$= £890$

Therefore, there is an **adverse** variance overall of £50.

This can be checked by adding the two separate variances together:

Rate variance	£(90)
Efficiency variance	£40
Overall variance	£(50)

(ii) Notice that adverse variances appear as **negative** figures.

iii) It is easy to get confused as to which figures to use – standard or actual. For the efficiency variance, note that **standard** as opposed to **actual** wage rate is used.

Possible causes for the variance:

(i) Adverse rate variance
- a pay rise may have been awarded, increasing average pay rates (this in itself might be due to a number of causes: competition for labour in the area, company bonus policy, or striking for higher wages)
- having to pay higher rates for more skilled workers

(ii) Favourable efficiency variance
- the workforce has been highly motivated
- the original standard time was set too high (i.e. a loose budget figure)
- more skilled workers have been employed

Notice that some reasons for a **favourable** efficiency variance are the same as the reasons for an **adverse** rate variance. For example, it may have been necessary to employ more skilled staff to operate sophisticated machinery; they work more efficiently, but want paying more.

Paying staff a bonus, or giving them a pay rise, may make them more motivated and hence more efficient. These variances may influence other factors in the organisation, such as how much raw material is wasted by production staff.

ACTIVITY

Can you think of any other possible causes for the variances shown above?

Can you think of other reasons how the rate variance and efficiency variance may be linked?

Load factor variances

These variances are used in several different situations. Load factor variances are often used to look at how well an asset is being used.

For example, for a bus on a particular route, an important measure is: how many passengers are normally carried?

The bus can seat 50 passengers. It has been calculated that it is only worth operating a particular route if the bus carries an average of 30 passengers or more.

Clearly, it is important that management knows whether this target is being met; otherwise, the bus company is losing money.

The 'load factor' in this case is **seat occupancy**.

This would normally be shown as a percentage:

	Budgeted
Seat occupancy (%)	60

(i.e. $\dfrac{50 \text{ total seats}}{30 \text{ budgeted occupied}} \times 100 = 60\%$)

If we compare this with the actual seat occupancy:

	Budgeted	*Actual*	*Variance*
Seat occupancy (%)	60	63	3 F

The bus is travelling with more passengers on average than expected. This is good news, so the variance is favourable (F).

Other examples of load factor variances include:

Load factor variance

Airline	Seat occupancy
Railways	Seat occupancy
Heavy goods lorry	Percentage of empty return journeys
Automated machine	Percentage of output damaged
Package holidays	Percentage of bookings per holiday
Hotel	Room occupancy rates

Each of these load factors will have a budgeted figure, against which actual performance can be measured.

Sometimes the budgeted figure will be one where the business just covers its costs. Referring to the bus example, if fewer than 30 passengers on average travel on each journey, the bus company loses money.

The budgeted figure can be set higher, however. If in the past, an average of 40 passengers travel on each journey, the new **standard** or **budgeted** figure should be around 40. (Refer back to the section on budgets if this is not clear.) Businesses want to make profit, not just cover their costs!

ACTIVITY

Can you discover any other load factor variances?

Note that you need to be careful when working out if a variance is favourable or adverse. This depends on how the variance is expressed.

For example:

	Budget	Actual	Variance
Machine output usable (%)	88	91	3 F

If the same results are expressed as:

	Budget	Actual	Variance
Machine output damaged (%)	12	9	3 F

The actual figure is 'lower' than the budgeted figure in the second case, but the variance is still **favourable**.

Overhead variances

Fixed overheads are absorbed **per unit** in absorption costing. This means that a variance can be caused by:

- spending too much (or little) on overheads
- producing too many (or too few) units

A simple example will illustrate this:

Budgeted output   400 units
Budgeted fixed overhead   £2000
Overhead absorption rate per unit is therefore:

$$\frac{2000}{400} = \text{£5 per unit}$$

Actual output   420 units
Actual fixed overhead incurred £2030

From these figures, three variances can be calculated:

Overhead expenditure variance

This is the difference between **budgeted** and **actual** fixed overheads:

£2000 – £2030 = £(30) ADVERSE

Notice that the negative value means the variance is adverse.

Overhead volume variance

This variance takes into account the fact that production levels may differ from budget, causing over- or under-absorption.

It is calculated by comparing **overhead absorbed using standard rate** with **budgeted fixed overhead**.

In the above example:

(£5 × 420) – £2000 = £100 FAVOURABLE

Notice that we have over-absorbed overhead, because production level *exceeded* the budgeted amount. An over-absorption means the true figure for overheads is lower, so it is favourable. (If you are unsure about this point, look back at the chapter dealing with under- and over-absorption.)

Total overhead variance

This variance combines the previous two variances. It compares **overhead absorbed using standard rate and actual production** with **actual overhead:**

$$(£5 \times 420) - £2030 = £70 \text{ FAVOURABLE}$$

To check this:

Overhead expenditure variance	£(30) A
Overhead volume variance	£100 F
Total overhead variance	£70 F

The three variances tell us that although we spent more on overheads than budgeted (£2030 as opposed to £2000 budgeted), this was more than offset by the higher production level (420 units as opposed to 400 budgeted). The result is an overall favourable variance.

ACTIVITY

Using the same budgeted and actual figures as in the previous example, calculate the expenditure, volume and total variances if actual production was **410 units**. Explain your answer.

PC 3
AN 3.2

■ Fixed overhead variances using labour hours

The variances calculated above are based on the number of units produced. It is possible to measure overhead variance based on the number of **labour hours worked**.

It is used when **labour hours worked** is used as an **absorption base** for absorbing fixed overhead.

An example:

Budgeted fixed overhead	£3000
Budgeted production (units)	300
Standard labour hours per unit	4

Standard fixed overhead absorption rate per labour hour is:

$$\frac{\text{Standard fixed overhead per unit}}{\text{Standard labour hours per unit}} = \frac{(3000/300)}{4} = £2.50$$

Actual hours worked were 1330
Actual units produced were 310

Fixed overhead efficiency variance

The formula for this variance is:

> **(Standard hours – actual hours) × standard fixed overhead absorption rate**

Note: 'Standard hours' is: no. of units actually produced × standard hours per unit.

In this example:

$$310 \times 4 = 1240$$

The variance is therefore:

$$(1240 - 1330) \times £2.50 = £(225) \text{ ADVERSE}$$

The units took longer to make than budgeted for, so there is an adverse variance.

Fixed overhead capacity variance

This variance looks at how much time was budgeted to be available for production, compared to how much time was *actually* spent. The formula for this variance is:

> **(Capacity used – budgeted capacity available) × standard fixed overhead absorption rate**

In the above example, the variance is:

$$(1330 - 1200) \times £2.50 = £325 \text{ FAVOURABLE}$$

Note: the figure of 1200 hours is used, because this is the number of hours **originally budgeted** for making this product, i.e. if standard labour hour and budgeted production were correct, 1200 hours should have been worked.

It is not immediately clear why this should be a 'favourable' variance. The reason is that many firms are limited by the amount of time available to make products; machines may be in full use, and shifts operating.

If the firm manages to use the production facilities for more hours, it may be avoiding machine stoppages or disrupted production. This represents a more efficient use of resources, and so is a **favourable** variance.

■ The link between variances

A variance in one area may be the cause of another variance. For example, a reduction in maintenance means lower overheads and a favourable overhead variance.

If the lack of maintenance causes machines to break down more often, there will be wasted labour time, resulting in an **adverse** labour efficiency variance.

■ Reporting variances

Variances provide useful information for managers. The reporting needs to be done on a regular, formal basis. It is usually part of the budgetary control system.

A typical variance report might look like this:

Variance report for the period ending 30th June 19xx

		£
Budgeted sales		13 000
Standard cost of budgeted sales		7 000
Budgeted gross profit		6 000
Add: favourable sales variances:		
Sales price variance	300	
Sales volume variance	130	430
Actual sales revenue less std cost of sales		6 430

Cost variances:	Adverse	Favourable	
Materials:			
Price	50		
Usage		13	
Labour:			
Rate	40		
Efficiency	68		
Fixed overhead:			
Expenditure		90	
Volume	46		
	204	103	Net (101) adverse
ACTUAL GROSS PROFIT			6329

Points to note

(i) This report includes sales variances; these work in a similar way to the cost variances we have studied.

(ii) The sum of all favourable and adverse variances are added together. The resulting figure of (£101) represents the **net** adverse variance.

Once prepared, the variance report will be circulated amongst the relevant managers. It is important to realise that the variance report does not exist to attribute blame to someone; it is there to help management constructively identify and solve problems.

ACTIVITY

Which managers do you think would be interested in each of the variances listed in the report?

Variance reports need to be issued frequently; in many businesses this is done weekly. Certain companies even issue daily variance reports. This gives management very rapid feedback. Computerisation has greatly helped in the rapid production of variance reports.

■ Illustrating variances as ratios

It is often helpful to show a variance as a ratio or percentage. A £70 variance from a budgeted £20 000 is not significant, whereas a £70 variance from a £200 budget *is* significant. Referring to a previous example:

Standard hours	= 3 hrs × 70 units
	= 210 hrs
Actual hours	= 200 hrs
Efficiency variance	= (210 – 200) × £4 (fixed overhead absorption rate)
	= £40 FAVOURABLE

The variance occurring is between **standard hours** and **actual hours** worked. To show this as a percentage:

$$\frac{\text{standard (210)}}{\text{actual (200)}} = 105\%$$

(It is not necessary to multiply both numbers by the £4 fixed overhead absorption rate.)

SUMMARY

1 **The difference between actual and budgeted performance is known as a variance.**

2 **These can be adverse or favourable.**

3 **Labour variances consider wage rate and how efficiently the work is done.**

4 **Overhead variances can arise by variances in spending on overheads, or by a variance in output.**

5 **Overhead variances can be based on labour hours, rather than output.**

6 **Variances are often linked – an adverse variance in one area can lead to a favourable variance in another area.**

7 **Management use variance reports to help determine why a variance has arisen.**

1 The following labour variances have been reported:

	Budgeted	Actual	Variance
Labour rate	£6	£4.50	£1.50 F
Labour efficiency	£300	£370	£(70) A

Suggest reasons why the two variances are like this.

2 For a company, the following overhead variances have been reported:

	Budgeted	Actual	Variance
Overhead expenditure	£3000	£2600	£400 F
Overhead volume	£3000	£2500	£500 A

The company had originally intended to buy some expensive machinery to boost production; the finance director argued against this. Suggest reasons why the company may have made the wrong decision.

14 Materials costing and stock valuation

Introduction

Stock needs to be valued so that final accounts can be prepared, and so that management have information for costing purposes. At first glance, valuing stock may appear easy. In practice, though, there are several different methods of stock valuation, each of which can give a different value.

■ SSAP 9

The rules which govern how businesses can value their stocks in published accounts are set out in SSAP 9. This will be referred to as we go through the chapter. It is important to remember that SSAP 9 only refers to **published** accounts; often a different valuation method may prove more useful for **internal** purposes (i.e. management use as an aid to decision making).

Cost and net realisable value

Cost is easy to define for stock in a shop. It is simply how much you paid for the stock, plus any transport or delivery expenses. In a manufacturing industry, though, there are costs other than the raw materials to produce the finished article. These are direct labour and a share of overheads, known as **conversion cost**. (This is an absorption costing approach – *see* Chapter 7.)

To summarise: In a retail/trading organisation:

> **Cost = Purchase price of stock + delivery costs**

In a manufacturing organisation:

> **Cost = Cost of raw materials + cost of direct labour**
> **+ share of overheads**

Net realisable value is the selling price of the stock, minus any selling and distribution expenses.

As you might expect, net realisable value is usually higher than cost.

ACTIVITY

Try to think of a situation where net realisable value is lower than cost.

When stock is obsolete, or damaged, it cannot be sold for what it cost. In such cases, net realisable value is lower than cost. Firms are required by SSAP 9 to value their stocks at the lower of cost or net realisable value. As cost is usually the lower, this will be examined in more detail.

Three different ways of measuring cost

If stock is valued at what the firm paid for it, this still presents problems. What if the price paid for stock changes through the year? Consider the following example:

Date	Units bought	Price	Units sold	Balance
1st Jan	100	£10		100
4th Mar	50	£11		150
6th May			100	50
12th Jun	150	£12		200
7th Sept			120	80
19th Nov	50	£12.50		130

Balance (no. of items in stock) at end of year = 130 units

As you can see, the price paid changed each time more stock was bought. There are several different stock valuations that can be calculated, depending on which price is chosen.

■ The FIFO method

FIFO stands for 'First In, First Out'. This method assumes that the stock bought earliest is the stock which gets sold first. In the above example, the stock bought in January will be sold before the units of stock bought in March, June or November. This means that the remaining stock was that bought most recently.

As there are 130 units remaining, this *must* include the 50 units bought in November. As this still leaves 80 units unaccounted for, these must be 80 of the 150 units bought in June (the next most recent purchase).

From this, it is possible to work out the value of the remaining stock:

50 units @ £12.50 each	£625
80 units @ £12 each	+ £960
Value of closing stock (using FIFO method)	**£1585**

■ The LIFO method

LIFO is short for 'Last In, First Out'. Unlike the previous method, LIFO assumes that the first stock that is sold is the most *recent* purchased. The stock left at the year end is the *oldest* stock.

In the example above, the 130 units of stock remaining must be the earliest purchased: 100 units bought in January and 30 of the 50 units bought in March.

Taking the cost prices of these units, the stock value is:

100 units @ £10 each	£1000
30 units @ £11 each	+ £330
Value of closing stock (using LIFO method)	**£1330**

ACTIVITY

Compare the different stock values given using the FIFO and LIFO methods. Which gives a more realistic picture?

■ AVCO

This method, also known as **cumulative weighted average pricing**, is a compromise between FIFO and LIFO. It calculates an **average** cost of a stock unit. The average can change with each reorder.

Using the above example:

Date units bought	No. units bought	Price	Units sold	Balance	Total stock val.	Unit cost
1st Jan	100	£10		100	£1000	£10
4th Mar	50	£11		150	£1550*	£10.33*
6th May			100	50	£516.67	£10.33
12th Jun	150	£12		200	£2316.67	£11.58
7th Sept			120	80	£926.67	£11.58
19th Nov	50	£12.50		130	£1551.67	£11.94

Closing stock valuation using AVCO method is £1551.67.

* Calculation:

Total stock value = (100 units × £10) + (50 units × £11)
= £1000 + £550
= £1550

(Average) unit cost = $\dfrac{£1550}{150 \text{ units}}$ = £10.33

Notice in the example that a new average is calculated every time new stock is **received**.

ACTIVITY

Why is a new average not calculated when stock is sold?

PC 2

ACTIVITY	PC 2
Produce a simple spreadsheet which will show the change in average unit cost each time new stock is bought.	IT 3.1
	IT 3.2
	AN 3.2
	AN 3.3

ACTIVITY

Produce a simple spreadsheet which will show the change in average unit cost each time new stock is bought.

If you are unsure how to calculate FIFO, LIFO and AVCO, go back through the chapter. If you understand, try Question 2 at the end of the chapter.

Under SSAP 9, both FIFO and AVCO are acceptable stock valuation methods. LIFO is not acceptable.

ACTIVITY

PC 2

Why do you think LIFO is not accepted as a method of valuing stocks in published accounts?

Replacement cost

It has been argued that for some businesses a different means of valuing stock is needed. This is **replacement cost**. As the name suggests, this is the cost of **replacing** stock by buying at **current prices.**

The advantage of this system is that it takes account of inflation. In a period of high inflation, where prices change rapidly, the value of stocks held is shown more accurately. The importance of this in decision making can be illustrated in the following example:

A wholesale company operates on low profit mark-ups of 10 per cent. It sells 100 units which cost £2 each when bought six months ago. What price should the units be sold for?

With a 10% mark-up:

(100 × 2) + 10% = £220

However, during the last six months high inflation has seen the cost of the units rise to £2.30 each.

To **replace** the 100 units sold will therefore cost the company:

100 × 2.30 = £230

It does not make sense to sell for £220 when you then have to pay £230 to replace the stock!

Replacement costing avoids this problem by giving an up-to-the-minute stock valuation on which to base selling price.

Replacement costing can be useful in a petrol company, which sells through its own garages. Here, the storage tanks are full of petrol which was bought at different costs throughout the year; it is very difficult to say how much the petrol 'cost' by referring to how much was paid when buying it. A much easier solution is to find the current (i.e. replacement) cost of buying the petrol.

Disadvantages of replacement costing are:

- it is not acceptable under SSAP 9
- sometimes it is not easy to determine the replacement cost

PC 2
AN 3.1

ACTIVITY

Try to find any business which uses replacement costing for internal accounting.

Valuing stock using absorption costing

FIFO, LIFO and AVCO are useful methods for valuing stock that is bought then sold, as in a retail or wholesale business. In both businesses, there is no work done on the stock.

In a manufacturing business, however, this is not an adequate approach. As mentioned in the introduction to this chapter, the stock consists of raw materials, on which money has been spent converting to finished goods (**conversion costs**).

For example, a carpenter buys planks of wood and produces a table. What is the value of the table?

Using an estimate of what we can sell the table for is not allowed. There is no guarantee it can be sold at that price!

The stock value of a product using absorption costing can be seen in this example:

	£
Raw materials (a direct cost)	10 000
Direct labour	12 000
Direct expenses	3 500
PRIME COST	25 500
Share of PRODUCTION overhead	8 500
FACTORY COST(= value of stock)	34 000

There are two important points to notice:

1. The value of the stock is the same as the **factory cost**.
2. Only **production** overhead is added to prime cost, in order to get a stock valuation – administrative, distribution and selling overheads are ignored.

The advantages of the absorption costing method of valuing stock are:

1. It takes into account conversion costs, not just raw materials.
2. By including a share of overheads (indirect costs) as well as direct costs, it helps management decide whether the product is making money or not.
3. Following on from advantage 2, it helps management decide a suitable selling price for the product.

ACTIVITY

How much is the conversion cost in the above example?

PC 2
AN 3.2

Valuing stock using marginal costing

Unlike absorption costing, marginal costing is only concerned with **variable** costs, and this applies to stock valuation using this method.

Using the same figures as in the absorption costing example, we can see the effect of adopting a marginal costing approach:

	£
Raw materials	10 000
Direct labour	12 000
Direct expenses	3 500
Variable production overheads*	1 700
Stock valuation(using marginal cost)	27 200

* Notice that there is no longer a share of *fixed* overheads, only the *variable* overheads, which increase as production increases – in this example £1700.

Don't confuse variable overheads with direct costs here. For example, if the company wants to increase production from 600 units to 610 units, it may need to rent a bigger warehouse. The rent increases from £2500/year to £3000/year. The variable overhead is therefore £500.

The rent has *varied* as the number of units has increased, and so is a *variable* overhead. (Remember that in marginal costing we are concerned with the 'extra' or 'marginal' cost of making *extra* units.) But the rent is not a **direct cost** to the particular product, because other products are stored in the warehouse as well.

In many cases, there might not be any variable overhead. As marginal costing ignores fixed costs (overhead), stock valuation is usually *lower* using marginal costing than using absorption costing.

For this reason, SSAP 9 states that companies must use an absorption costing approach when valuing stock in their published accounts.

PC 2
AN 3.2

ACTIVITY

What would be the effect on published profits of showing a lower stock valuation (e.g. by using marginal costing)?

SUMMARY

1 **There are several different ways of valuing stock.**

2 **SSAP 9 governs which stock valuation methods companies use in their published accounts.**

3 **Net realisable value can sometimes be lower than cost.**

4 **FIFO stands for 'First in, First out'.**

5 **LIFO stands for 'Last in, First out'.**

6 **The AVCO method of stock valuation is a compromise between the LIFO and FIFO methods.**

7 **Replacement cost is useful where a single product is sold, which varies frequently in cost. It is not acceptable under SSAP 9.**

8 **SSAP 9 states that companies can use absorption costing to value stocks, but not marginal costing.**

QUESTIONS

1 A fashion company paid £13 000 for the stock left on the shelves at the year end. The sales director thinks that the company may have difficulty selling the stock, as fashion has changed since the stock was bought. Should the stock appear in the published accounts at £13 000 or at a different figure?

PC 2
AN 3.2

PC 2
AN 3.2

2 Date	Units bought	Price	Units sold	Balance
1/3	70	£3		70
2/3			20	50
6/3	40	£3.30		90
9/3			30	60
12/3	50	£3.10		110
13/3		45		65
16/3	40	£2.80		105
24/3			25	80

Calculate the value of the closing stock for the month using:
(i) FIFO
(ii) LIFO
(iii) AVCO methods

15 Pricing

Determining what price to charge for its products is one of the most important decisions a firm can make. The essential point in deciding price is that costs must be covered. By charging less than the cost, a loss will be made.

The difficulty in pricing occurs when deciding *what* costs to include. As we have seen, different costing techniques, such as absorption costing or marginal costing, result in different unit costs for a product. If the unit cost is then used as a basis for determining the selling price, it is possible to arrive at several different answers for the same product.

PC 4 Methods of pricing

■ Mark-up

The most common method of pricing, a fixed percentage is added on to the cost of a product to arrive at a unit selling price:

	£
Unit cost	8
add: 50% mark-up	4
Selling price	12

The percentage added on to cost is referred to as the **mark-up**, and represents the gross profit on selling a unit. Notice that the mark-up is always expressed as **a percentage of cost**, not a percentage of selling price.

The advantages of mark-up pricing are that:

- it is quick and easy to calculate
- it allows selling price to be determined for a range of products

The disadvantages are:

- a suitable mark-up percentage to cover fixed costs may be difficult to determine when using marginal costing
- setting a price using mark-up percentage does not mean that the product can be sold at that price

■ Cost-plus pricing

As the name suggests, **cost-plus pricing** is a method where the desired profit is added on to the costs of a project.

It is typically used where a firm undertakes a large project for the Government. The best examples of cost-plus pricing occur in the defence industry.

Looking at one such example will help to understand the nature of cost-plus accounting:

The Government decides to order a nuclear submarine to be built. Because nuclear submarines are so expensive and complex, very few shipyards are capable of building them. This means that the Government isn't able to 'shop around' to find who will supply a submarine at the cheapest price. For a shipyard to bid for the contract to build a submarine, it would need a lot of information. However, this information is top secret and can't be released to several different shipyards.

Therefore, the Government appoints a shipyard to build the submarine.

In a normal contract, the firm would quote a price and hope to complete the project for less than this amount. The difference between cost and quoted price would be its profit.

In the case of a new nuclear submarine, though, it is often impossible to estimate the costs involved. If the technology is new and untested, costs could be much greater than initially estimated.

A consequence of being unable to predict costs is that a firm would be very foolish to accept such a contract! The risk of costs escalating are very high.

To encourage firms to take on such risky projects, the government *guarantees* to pay the costs, *and* pay the firm extra money (i.e. the firm's profit).

In practice, the government will determine a suitable **rate of return** for the firm. This will reflect how much capital the firm has tied up in the project, and for how long it is tied up.

The benefits of such cost-plus pricing are:

- the government is able to have private firms undertake complex projects.
- the firm can be guaranteed a profit on the project

However, cost-plus pricing has a number of weaknesses:

- The firm undertaking the work is under no pressure to cut costs, as profit is guaranteed. Waste and inefficiency can occur, which the taxpayer has to pay for.
- It is open to abuse by firms arbitrarily apportioning a high share of overhead costs to a project.

■ Market-led pricing

This method of pricing puts less emphasis on the **cost** of a product, instead looking at how much a product can be *sold for.*

This will depend on numerous factors, such as the state of the market or the level of competition.

Market-led pricing can work to a business's advantage. Where customer demand exceeds production of a product, the price can be raised; there will still be enough customers at the new, higher price.

For example, a firm sells a product costing £5 to make. It plans to sell it at £10 (a 100 per cent mark-up). However, demand is such that it can charge £12 for the product and still sell all it makes. At which price should the product be sold?

The answer is obviously £12. Selling it at any less involves a missed opportunity to make higher profits; there is an **opportunity cost** of £2 if the product is only sold at £10.

In many cases, however, market-led pricing is to the business's disadvantage. Due to lack of demand for its products, the business can only charge £9 instead of the planned £10.

PC 4

ACTIVITY

What would be the consequence of the business still pricing its products at £10 instead of £9?

In both cases, the selling price of the product is not determined by the business, but by the market. It is therefore *market-led*. The business sells its products priced at 'what the market will bear'; the highest price at which the business can still sell all its production.

Market-led pricing is an example of the economic laws of supply and demand, which state that ultimately it is the **consumer** who determines the price of products.

Other pricing considerations

■ Loss leaders

Some businesses sell certain products at **less than cost** as a way of attracting customers. Such items are known as **loss leaders**. This is typically done by supermarkets, who may advertise low priced baked beans or petrol to attract custom.

■ Obsolete stock

When stock has become out-of-date or obsolete, it is unlikely that the business will be able to sell it at normal prices. The stock will have to be sold for whatever the business can get for it, even if this means making a loss. This is another form of market-led pricing.

Clothes stores, which rely on stocking up-to-the-minute fashion items, often find themselves with old stock, which they dispose of by holding sales (often with large price reductions).

■ Market share and promotion

A business may want to grow by increasing its **market share** (what percentage of the market for a product it supplies). One way of doing this is to have a short-term price reduction on a product. Given the choice between similar products at different prices, people will usually buy the cheaper product.

It can be a disadvantage to firms to sell a product at a lower than normal price. Customers who would have bought the product anyway might buy the product at the new, lower price. In other words, the number of customers has not significantly increased, but profit margins have been cut – not a very beneficial situation. Furthermore, a firm risks upsetting its regular customers if it starts selling products for less than they have just paid!

A promotion usually applies to a new product. In order to get people to try the product, it may initially be sold at a price lower than cost. Typical examples of this are new chocolate bars.

For both market share and promotion, the low price is a temporary measure, designed to improve the business's sales and hence profits in the longer term.

PC 4

ACTIVITY

Try to find at least one example of: promotion; market share pricing; loss leader; obsolete stock.

SUMMARY

1 Deciding what costs to include when calculating unit cost is difficult.

2 The mark-up method adds a fixed percentage on to the unit cost.

3 Cost-plus pricing often guarantees a profit for the company. It can lead to inefficiency.

4 Market-led pricing focuses on what people are willing to pay for a product.

5 **Loss leaders are designed to attract customers to the shop.**

6 **Obsolete stock often has to be sold at less than cost.**

7 **Promotions aim to attract new customers for a product.**

QUESTION

Complete the gaps in this table:

PC 4
AN 3.2

Cost (£)	15	20	3000				30
Mark-up %	20	75	100	50	100	25	
Selling price (£)				18	400	500	40

Element 11.3 Assignment

Scenario

Kirkstall Ltd is a medium-sized engineering company, making specialised drilling equipment. You have recently joined the company as a junior cost accountant.

PC 1
AN 3.1

Task 1

The company uses an absorption costing method for costing and pricing its products. Only production overheads are included in the calculation of unit cost. The following costs have been identified – you have to classify them into production or non-production overheads.

	£
Factory rent	7000
Promotions	1450
Advertising	4600
Salaries:	
office staff	16 000
factory staff	23 000
directors	13 200
Fleet transport maintenance	4640
Warehousing	3390
Maintenance department – machinery	6700
Loan interest	9950
Canteen	6000

PC 1
PC 2
AN 3.2
C 3.2

Task 2

The company makes two products: Titan drills and Eureka drill casings. You have to calculate the unit cost for each product.

The following additional information about the company is available:

	Product	
	Titan	*Eureka casing*
Standard material usage(kg)	3	11
Standard time (hrs)	4	8
Budgeted production	400	200
Standard machine hrs	1.5	9

Standard material price(kg)	£17
Standard wage rate (per hr)	£4.80
Canteen overhead	£6000
Overhead solely related to production	£17 000

Department	Production	Admin.	Sales	Total
No. of employees	40	15	5	60

Both products are made on a very expensive piece of machinery which is kept operating 24 hours a day.

Write your results in a memo to the chief cost accountant. You should also explain why you have chosen the basis of apportionment used.

Task 3

PC 4
AN 3.2
C 3.2
C 3.3

The company originally planned to sell the products at unit cost plus a 50 per cent mark-up. However, due to current market conditions, the products can only be sold at these prices:

Titan drills	£95
Eureka drill casings	£270

You have been asked by management to produce a report advising whether production of one or both of the products should be continued.

Task 4

PC 3
AN 3.2
C 3.2

Kirkstall Ltd have recently undergone major changes. New (and very expensive) mechanised production methods have been introduced, placing new demands on production staff. They have had to learn new skills and to adapt quickly to the new machinery. There has been some disquiet among staff over this, and a feeling that their workload has increased. Some of the most skilled staff have taken early retirement or voluntary redundancy.

The management, on the other hand, feel they have done what they can for the workers, including giving extra training.

The following variances have been noted:

	Budget	Actual	Variance
Raw materials usage	3 kg	2.9 kg	0.1 kg F
Raw materials price	£17/kg	£19.70/kg	£(2.70) A
Labour wage rate	£4.80	£4.45	£0.35 F
Labour efficiency	800 hrs	790 hrs	10 hrs F

Explain in a memo to a colleague what you think the causes for the variances are.

Element 11.4

INVESTIGATE HOW ORGANISATIONS USE FINANCIAL INFORMATION TO ASSESS PERFORMANCE AND MAKE DECISIONS

PERFORMANCE CRITERIA

1 **Information required for monitoring and decision-making are identified**
   Range: sales, production, staffing, internal/external sources, limitations

2 **Appropriate techniques are selected**
   Range: break-even analysis, make or buy decisions, capital investment
   appraisal

3 **Appropriate recommendations are made from analysis of data**

4 **Recommendations are justified at planning meetings**

EVIDENCE INDICATORS

The preparations of a briefing paper for a meeting at which the decision to approve/not approve a project is made. The preparation involved collection of information, application of techniques and justification for decision.

16 Break-even analysis

Businesses often use break-even analysis as a means of assessing a single product. When considering whether to make or sell a particular item, it is useful to know two things:

PC 1

- How many do we need to sell to cover our costs (i.e. to break even)?
- What will our profit be for a given level of sales?

Break-even analysis allows us to calculate both of these.

It is a form of marginal costing, and so fixed costs and variable costs are treated separately.

To recap what was covered in a previous chapter, the costs and revenues involved are:

- **Fixed costs**. These do not change with level of output.
- **Variable costs**. These *do* change with output (level of sales). For the purposes of break-even analysis, the variable costs need to be shown as **variable cost per unit**.
- **Selling price**. This is simply the price *per unit*.
- **Contribution per unit**. This is **the difference between selling price and variable cost per unit**.

The break-even point

PC 2

The **break-even point** is the **number of units** we need to sell to **cover fixed costs.** It is the point at which:

Total revenue = fixed costs + variable costs.

However, a more useful way to show this is to express it in terms of contribution:

Break-even point occurs when **fixed costs = total contribution**.

> Therefore, break-even point = $\dfrac{\text{Fixed costs}}{\text{Unit contribution}}$

A simple example will show this:

Fairline Ltd make golf clubs. The golf clubs sell for £8 each. Direct materials cost £3 per club, and direct labour a further £3 per club. The fixed costs are £4600 per year. How many clubs do Fairline Ltd have to sell to break even?

Variable cost per club = £3 + £3 = £6
Unit contribution = £8 − £6 = £2

$$\text{Break-even point} = \frac{£4600}{£2}$$

$$= 2300 \text{ units}$$

If Fairline Ltd sell this number of golf clubs, they will have exactly covered their fixed costs.

ACTIVITY

Discuss what would happen if Fairline Ltd sold 2301 clubs.

■ Calculating expected profit

This uses the same principles as finding the break-even point. In this case, however, the sales revenue will be greater than the total costs.

Using contribution:

> **Profit = total contribution − fixed costs**

In the above example, what would be Fairline Ltd's profit if they sold 3000 clubs?

Total contribution = unit contribution × no. of units

$$= £2 \times 3000$$
$$= £6000$$

Profit $= £6000 - £4600$
$= £1400$

AN 3.2

ACTIVITY

Calculate Fairline Ltd's profit if they sell:
(i)   2400 clubs
(ii) 4000 clubs
(iii) 5500 clubs

■ Calculating break-even point using a graph

Figure 16.1 shows a graphical treatment of break-even point:.

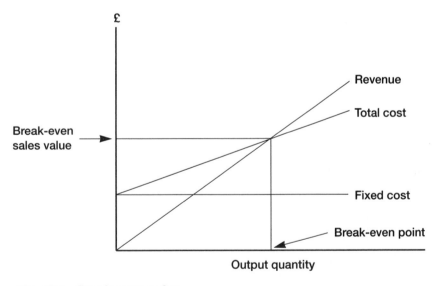

Fig. 16.1   Break-even point

There are several points to notice from the graph. First, notice how the
fixed costs appear as a horizontal line. This is because they stay the same
whatever the quantity of output.

Second, notice how the **total costs** line rises with increased output. This is because total costs consists of both fixed *and* variable costs.

The **total revenue** line simply shows the amount of money coming in from sales. Where this crosses the **total cost** line marks break-even.

Break-even can be shown in two ways on the graph:

- The break-even point. This is shown on the horizontal axis, and is the **number of units** at which the firm breaks even.
- The break-even sales value. This is on the vertical axis, and states how much in pounds the firm needs from sales to just cover costs.

Both occur at the same time, but it is important that you understand the difference.

AN 3.3

ACTIVITY

To better understand the relationship between the various cost and revenue lines, complete the following table:

Selling price per unit: £10
Variable cost per unit: £6

Sales(units)	Total revenue	Fixed cost	Variable cost	Total cost
0	0	2000	0	2000
200				
400				
600				
800				
1000				
1200				
1400				
1600				

When you have done this, plot the following lines on a graph:
    Total revenue
    Fixed cost
    Total cost
Mark on the break-even point and break-even sales value.

Calculating profit from the break-even graph

This is easily done. Look at the graph in Fig. 16.2.

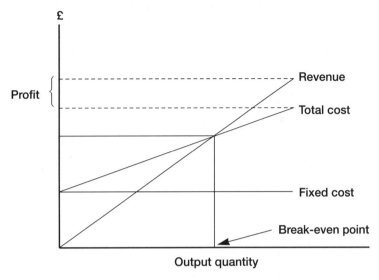

Fig. 16.2   Calculating profit from a break-even graph

The profit for any level of sales is the difference between total revenue and total costs. By drawing a vertical line up from the particular sales level on the horizontal axis, the gap between **total revenue** and **total cost** can be measured – this is **profit**. (If **total revenue** is less than **total cost**, then the business is making a loss.)

This is a very useful technique, as a business can see at a glance how much profit will be made for any level of sales.

The contribution/fixed cost graph

A simpler way of showing break-even graphically is to plot a contribution against fixed cost graph (*see* Fig. 16.3).

Break-even on the graph occurs where the **contribution line** crosses the **fixed cost** line. As you can see, there are only two lines that have to be drawn with this method, so there is less risk of making a mistake.

A further advantage of this graph is that the break-even point is much clearer. Normal break-even graphs often have **total cost** and **total revenue** lines meeting at a shallow angle, and it is not possible to tell the exact cross-over point.

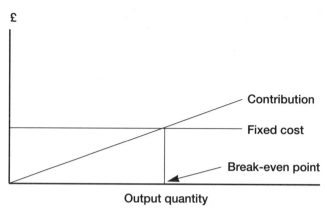

Fig. 16.3 Contribution/fixed cost graph

Safety margins

The **margin of safety** is defined as:

> the difference between **budgeted sales** and **break-even sales**.

Here is a simple example:

Jacobson Ltd sell Cracklets. The estimated sales are 4000 units per year. Break-even number of sales is 3000 units per year.

Safety margin = estimated sales – break-even number sales
= 4000 – 3000
= 1000 units

It is more helpful to express this as a percentage:

$$\text{Safety margin} = \frac{(4000 - 3000)}{4000 \text{ (budgeted sales)}} \times 100\% = 25\%$$

What does the safety margin mean? It represents **how much sales can fall by without making a loss**.

In the above example, sales of Cracklets can drop by 1000, or 25 per cent, and Jacobsons Ltd will still make some profit.

If sales fall by **more than 25 per cent**, the company will make a loss.

The safety margin is very useful in decision making. Consider the following two products:

	Product	
	PH	TM
Expected profit (at sales target)	£100	£130
Safety margin	50%	15%

The company has to decide which of the two products to make. Product TM gives higher profit, but *only if* sales reach their target.

What if sales don't reach target? There is only a small (15 per cent) safety margin with product TM, whereas product PH is much safer to make, having a 50 per cent safety margin.

In such circumstances, the company may choose to make product PH; it is better to be safe, even if some potential profit is sacrificed.

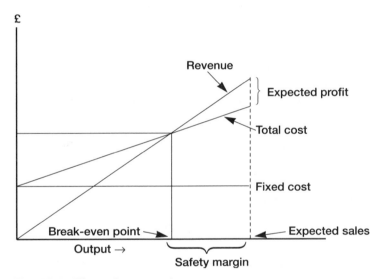

Fig. 16.4 The safety margin

■ The limitations of break-even analysis

PC 1

Break-even analysis gives a simple, visual indication of the level of sales needed to cover fixed costs in a business. There are several important drawbacks to break-even analysis, however. These are:

- It can only be used for a single product, with a standard selling price.
- It assumes that costs increase in a **linear** fashion. In practice, economies of scale may mean costs do not rise as fast as output.
- It assumes fixed costs stay constant, irrespective of level of output.

SUMMARY

1 Break-even analysis looks at the level of sales needed to cover fixed costs.

2 Break-even point = fixed costs/unit contribution.

3 Profit = total contribution – fixed costs.

4 Break-even can be shown graphically.

5 A contribution against fixed costs graph is simpler and quicker to produce than a normal break-even graph.

6 The safety margin is an indication of how much forecast sales can fall before the business makes a loss.

7 Limitations with break-even analysis include: only suitable for a single product; assuming costs stay fixed; assuming contribution stays constant with changing output.

QUESTION

The following information for a product is available:

Selling price	£36
Variable costs per unit:	
raw materials	£7.50
labour	£12.50
packaging	£3
Fixed costs:	£4000 per year

Plot a graph to show:
(i)   expected profit
(ii) break-even sales volume
(iii) break-even sales value
(iv) margin of safety

ASSIGNMENT

AN 3.2
AN 3.3
C 3.2
C 3.3

Wally has decided to set up a pizza parlour. He has asked you, as a friend, for financial advice.

Wally has estimated the following figures for the proposed business:

Selling price per pizza £7
Costs

rent	£3200/year
gas and electric	£900/yr
rates	£1800/yr
wages	£90/week
pizza dough	£12 per order (enough for 10 pizzas)
topping	£1.30 per pizza
boxes for pizzas	£50 per 100

He is also hoping to pay himself a salary of £9000 in the first year.

Task 1

PC 2
PC 3

Advise Wally as to how many pizzas he will need to sell to:
a) break even
b) pay himself the £9000 salary

Task 2

PC 1

Explain in a letter to Wally what the limitations are of using break-even analysis in this situation.

17 Make or buy decisions

A common question facing a cost accountant is whether it is better for a company to buy a product or component from an outside supplier, or make it itself. Using marginal costing techniques can help the accountant to arrive at a decision.

PC 2 Make or buy calculations

Where a company buys in components from an outside supplier, the cost is purely direct (i.e. marginal). If the company decides to make the component itself the costs will be **direct** material and labour costs, together with variable production overheads.

There will also be some fixed costs incurred. Because make or buy uses **marginal costing** techniques, we are only interested in those fixed costs which are **directly attributable** to a particular component. For example, the rent for a factory would need to be paid whether one small component was made or not. If an extra factory unit had to be rented, just to make that component, then the fixed cost *would be directly attributable* to that component.

To appreciate this, look at this worked example:

Glendale Ltd make three components at present. The company needs to decide whether it is better to buy any of these components in.

Component	A	B	C
Production (units per annum)	1000	2500	500
Marginal (direct) costs per unit:	£	£	£
direct materials	4	9	6
direct labour	12	3	18
variable production o/hds	3	2	8
DIRECT COST PER UNIT	19	14	32

Fixed costs incurred (per annum)

	£
Directly related to A:	3000
Directly related to B:	1800
Directly related to C:	2000

Glendale Ltd have been quoted the following prices for components by suppliers:

Component A	£18.50
Component B	£15
Component C	£34

By comparing these prices to the direct cost of manufacturing, we can see at a glance that it is cheaper to buy in Component A: £18.50 to buy in against £19 direct cost to manufacture.

Components B and C have lower **direct** manufacturing costs than buying in, but the **fixed costs** need also to be considered.

Component	A	B	C
	£	£	£
Direct cost of making	19	14	32
No. of units annually	1 000	2 500	500
Annual direct cost	19 000	35 000	16 000
Fixed costs	3 000	1 800	2 000
Total annual cost of making	22 000	36 800	18 000
Direct cost of buying per unit	18.50	15	34
Total annual cost of buying (i.e. direct cost × annual no.)	18 500	37 500	17 000
Money saved by buying	3 500	(700)	1 000

Having taken fixed costs into account, it is clear that the company will save money if it buys in Components A and C. Component B is still cheaper to make than buy.

This calculation can also be done more quickly by comparing the difference in direct cost between making and buying:

	A £	B £	C £
Direct cost of making	19	14	32
Direct cost of buying	18.50	15	34
Extra variable cost of buying per unit	(0.50)	1	2
No. of units annually	1000	2500	500
Extra variable cost of buying per annum	(500)	2500	1000
Fixed costs per annum saved by buying	3000	1800	2000
Savings made by buying	3500	(700)	1000

PC 2

■ Make or buy and limiting factors

In some instances, it may appear cheaper for a business to make components rather than buy in, and yet the business buys in. This occurs where there is a **limiting factor**.

An example of this is shown below:

Belshazzar Inc. make three components:

Component	Nut	Bolt	Washer
Budgeted production	200	200	200
Machine hours per unit	4	2	3
Variable cost per unit	£2.40	£3.60	£2.00

There is only limited time available on the machine of 1100 hours.

Hours required to make budgeted production:

Component	Nut	Bolt	Washer
	(200 × 4)	(200 × 2)	(200 × 3)
	= 800	= 400	= 600
Total hours reqd			1800

As there are only 1100 machine hours available, some components will have to be bought in.

The following prices have been quoted for buying in the components:

Nut £3.40   Bolt £4.00   Washer £2.90

Machine hours are a **limiting factor** here. What we need to decide is which component(s) are cheapest to buy in **per machine hour**?

We use 'per machine hour' because *all* components are more expensive to buy in than manufacture. We need to use the machine to its best efficiency, by producing those components which would otherwise be the most expensive to buy in.

To calculate this:

Component	Nut	Bolt	Washer
Variable cost of making	£2.40	£3.60	£2.00
Variable cost of buying	£3.40	£4.00	£2.90
Extra(vble)cost of buying	1.00	0.40	0.90
Mach. hrs saved by buying	4	2	3
Extra cost per machine hour of buying	1.00/4 = 25p	0.40/2 = 20p	0.90/3 = 30p

From this, we can see that it would be *most* expensive to buy in washers (30p per machine hour extra cost), and cheapest to buy in bolts at 20p per machine hour extra cost.

As there are only 1100 machine hours available, these should be used as follows:

600 hours to make washers (3 hrs × 200 washers budgeted prodn)
500 hours (1100 – 600 already used) to make nuts

In 500 hours, only 500/4 = 125 nuts can be made. Therefore, the company needs to buy in:

75 nuts (200 – 125 made)
200 bolts

■ Non-financial considerations

The choice of whether to make or buy a component can depend on factors other than cost.

These factors are:

Quality

It may be easier to maintain quality control if the component is produced 'in-house' than bought in, for example. Every stage in production can be checked using the firm's own standards, and potentially costly failures of components may be avoided.

Reliability of supply

If the supplier is not reliable in delivering the component, the whole production process could be held up, resulting in losses far greater than the initial cost saving.

Space

Although a component might be made for less than it can be bought, the factory space could be used more productively in making something else.

Capital

If capital is in short supply, making components may mean using up capital to purchase new machinery for this, even though there is a cost saving. The capital could be used more productively elsewhere.

The previous two factors are examples of **opportunity cost**. It is often hard to put a figure on opportunity cost, and decisions to make or buy often rest on a manager's judgement. Despite this, cost accounting can give useful information to help make this decision.

ACTIVITY

Can you think of any other examples of opportunity cost in deciding whether to make or buy a component?

SUMMARY

1 Make or buy decisions involve using marginal costing.

2 Limiting factors, such as machine hours available, can result in buying in even where it appears cheaper to make a product.

3 There are non-financial considerations when deciding to make or buy. These include: quality; reliability of supply; space; capital.

QUESTION

PC 1
PC 2
PC 3
AN 3.2
C 3.2

Goldrise Ltd make a single product. At present the company manufactures three components, for which the following budget estimates are available:

Component	X	Y	Z
Annual production (units)	500	1000	800
	£	£	£
Direct materials	7 500	16 000	8 800
Direct labour	2 500	4 000	2 400
Variable overheads	1 500	10 000	4 000
Direct costs	11 500	30 000	15 200
Share of fixed overheads	2 000	800	1 200

The fixed overheads are machinery costs and factory rent used only for producing the three components.

A potential supplier has been found, who has quoted the following prices per unit:

  X £19   Y £32   Z £16

There will also be additional storage charges if bought in. These are annually:

  X £2500   Y £3000   Z £3200

Prepare a report for management showing which if any of the components should be bought in. Your report should also refer to any other factors which management should consider in reaching their decision.

(*Note to student:* In this question, there are fixed costs associated with buying in the components.)

18 Investment appraisal

Introduction

Imagine yourself in this situation. You have to decide whether or not to buy a piece of machinery. It costs £40 000, and will reduce expenses by £5000 a year. Should you buy it? This is a very common situation in business – every time a computer, piece of machinery, or new vehicle is bought, the initial cost has to be compared with the expected savings (or profit increase).

Investment appraisal helps managers make decisions about buying capital items. (Capital items are things a business buys which it hopes to use over a few years. They are different from stock or consumables, which change from day to day.)

PC 2

There are four main methods of investment appraisal:

- Payback period
- Accounting rate of return
- Net present value
- Internal rate of return

Payback period

This simply calculates how long before the investment pays for itself. For example:

A computer is purchased for £2400. The estimated savings are as follows:

Year 1   £1000
2   £800
3   £600
4   £600

The computer pays for itself in **3 years** (i.e. £1000 + 800 +600); it recoups the original cost of £2400.

Calculating payback period accurately

Purchase machine for £10 000.

Cash flows generated by investment:

Yr 1   £4000
Yr 2   £5000
Yr 3   £4000
Yr 4   £3000

The machine pays for itself at some stage between the end of the second year and the end of the third year. To see how this is calculated:

(i) Add the cash flows for each year together.
Thus, after year 2, £4000 + £5000 = £9000 has been paid back. After year 3, £4000 + £5000 + £4000 = £13 000 has been paid back. Therefore, as the machine cost £10 000, it paid for itself during the third year.

(ii) To get a more accurate figure, *subtract* total paid back in preceding year from **cost of investment**. In this case, £10 000 – £9000 (amount paid back to date at end of preceding year) = £1000

This figure is used to divide the amount paid back in the year in which the machine *finishes* paying for itself (i.e. Yr 3 in our example).

$$\frac{£1000}{£4000} = 0.25$$

Adding this onto 2 years, we get 2.25 years; this is the time the machine takes to pay for itself.

To show this as a formula, we'll call the year in which the investment finally pays for itself the 'payback year'.

$$\text{Payback period} = \text{no. of yrs before payback year} +$$

$$\frac{\text{amount still to pay back}}{\text{cash received in payback year}}$$

Note: The payback method uses **cashflow** rather than **profit**.

ACTIVITY

Discuss why cashflow rather than profit is used.

AN 3.2

ACTIVITY

A new computer system is purchased costing £3800. The expected savings resulting from the purchase are:

Year 1	£800
Year 2	£1200
Year 3	£1200
Year 4	£1000
Year 5	£900

The system is worthless at the end of five years.

Calculate the payback period.

PC 1
PC 2

Advantages of the payback method
- It is simple to calculate.
- It gives greater prominence to cashflow in the early years. This is particularly important for businesses where cashflow is tight.
- By concentrating on the near future, the figures used are more reliable than, say, estimates of cashflow in seven or eight years time.

Limitations of the payback method
- It ignores the 'time value' of money. To understand this, you need to appreciate that £1 paid to you in, say, three years time, is not worth as much as £1 is today. This is a major limitation of the payback method.
- It ignores future profits, being only concerned with the point at which the investment pays for itself. To get round this problem, we use the following method.

Accounting Rate of Return (ARR)

(*Note:* This is sometimes referred to as Average Rate of Return.) Unlike the payback method, Accounting Rate of Return takes into account future profits. Using the previous example:

A firm purchases a machine for £10 000. Cash flows generated by investment:

Yr 1	£4000
Yr 2	£5000
Yr 3	£4000
Yr 4	£3000
Total:	£16 000

The Accounting Rate of Return is calculated using this formula:

$$ARR = \left(\frac{\text{Total profit}}{\text{No. of years}} \right) / \text{Cost of investment} \times 100$$

In the above example:

$$ARR = \left(\frac{16\ 000 - 10\ 000}{4} \right) / £10\ 000 \times 100$$

$$= 1500/10\ 000 \times 100$$

$$= 15\%$$

The figure of 15 per cent means that for every £1 invested, we receive £1 plus 15p profit ('return') back.

AN 3.2

ACTIVITY

Using the figures in the previous activity, calculate the Accounting Rate of Return for the computer system.

■ Disadvantage of accounting rate of return method

Accounting Rate of Return ignores the *timing* of the cash flows. To understand this, consider this situation:

	Machine A	Machine B
	£	£
Year 1	3000	500
2	4000	500
3	2000	4000
4	800	4800
	9800	9800

Both machines have the same Accounting Rate of Return, having identical returns in total. However, Machine A receives most cash back before Machine B, and is therefore a better buy.

Discounted cashflow techniques

PC 1
PC 2

■ The time value of money

Given the choice between £100 now or £100 in a year's time, most people would choose to have £100 now. Apart from the risk of not getting it in a year's time, with £100 now, you could spend it or put it in a building society savings account.

- By spending the money now, you are getting more than you would in a year's time, because prices rise.
- By putting the money in a savings account, you will receive interest on your money.

In either case, you are better receiving the money now!

However, let's look at a slightly different situation. You have the choice between having £100 now, and putting it in a savings account with 10 per cent interest, *or* £110 in a year's time.

Which is better?

In one year's time, £100 + 10% interest (i.e. £10 a year) = £110

In other words, there is no difference! £100 *now* is the same as £110 in one *year's time*. £110 in one year's time is *equivalent to* £100 in today's money.

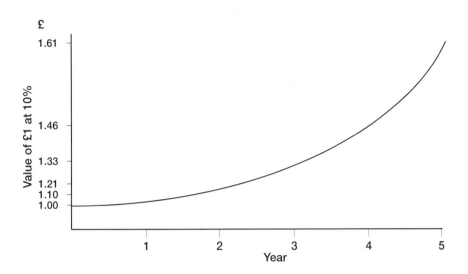

Fig. 18.1 Discounted cashflow. In the above diagram, receiving £1.61 in five years' time is *the same* as receiving £1 now (assuming 10 per cent interest).

AN 3.2
AN 3.3

ACTIVITY

What if the interest in the savings account was
a) 5%
b) 15%?

If the choice was between £100 now, or an *equivalent* amount in two years' time, how much would you want? (Assuming the interest rate is still 10 per cent.)

   £100 after one year + 10% interest = £110
   After two years = £110 + 10% interest = £121

Notice that the interest in year 2 is £11, not £10. This is because you receive 10% per cent of £110, not £100.

The equivalent amount after three years' time of £100 now would be:

Now	£100
After 1 year	£100 + £10 interest = £110
After 2 years	£110 + £11 interest = £121
After 3 years	£121 + £12.10 interest = £133.10

Continuing for the next few years:

After 4 years £133.10 + £13.31 interest = £146.41
After 5 years £146.41 + £14.64 interest = £161.05

PC 2
AN 3.2

Notice how quickly the amount grows. This is known as **compounding**.

> ## ACTIVITY
>
> What would £100 be worth after
>
> a) 6 years
> b) 7 years?
>
> How long would it be before the original £100 doubled in amount?

With **compounding**, we are asking: what will £1 be worth in a few years' time?

In practice, though, we estimate how much money we will be receiving. What we need to know is: **how much is that money worth in today's money?**

A simple example:

> You have been promised £100 in a year's time, or **the equivalent amount** today. How much would that be? Firstly, you would be happy with *less* than £100 today! This is because you can put the amount in a savings account, and earn interest on it.

PC 2
AN 3.2

> ## ACTIVITY
>
> If interest rates are 10 per cent, how much money would you need to end up with £100 in one year's time?

The answer, surprisingly, is £90.90! It is not £90 exactly, because adding 10 per cent on to £90 will give:

£90 + £9 (i.e. 10% of £90) = £99

If we had been promised £100 in two years' time, or the equivalent in today's money, we would need:

£82.60 (approximately!)
To check this: £82.60 + 10% (i.e. £8.26) = £90.86
£90.86 + 10% (i.e. £9.09) = £99.95

This is near enough to £100 (to get the exact figure, we would have to use many decimal places).

These figures, unlike compounding, are difficult to work out by just using a calculator. Fortunately, the figures are available in tables, which make calculation easier. These tables are known as **discount factor tables**, and show what **£1 received in a few years' time** is worth **in today's money**.

Table of factors for the present value of £1

Year	8%
1	0.926
2	0.857
3	0.794
4	0.735
5	0.681

How much would £350 received in four years' time be worth in today's money?

£350 × 0.735 (the discount factor for year 4)
= £239.05

Notice it is worth *less* in today's money!

ACTIVITY

Using the 8% discount factor table, what would £620 received in

a) 2 years' time
b) 5 years' time

be worth in today's money?

PC 2
AN 3.2

The discount factors shown so far are only correct for a particular interest rate (8%). Each interest rate has its own table of discount factors – *see* Appendix, page 178.

Table of factors for the present value of £1

Year	11%	12%	14%	16%	20%
1	0.901	0.893	0.877	0.862	0.833
2	0.812	0.797	0.769	0.743	0.694
3	0.731	0.712	0.675	0.641	0.579
4	0.659	0.636	0.592	0.552	0.482
5	0.594	0.567	0.519	0.476	0.402

PC 2
AN 3.2

ACTIVITY

Using the discount tables above, what would
a) £750 received in 4 years' time at 14% be worth?
b) £750 received in 4 years' time at 16% be worth?
c) £750 received in 4 years' time at 20% be worth?

Notice how the higher the interest rate, the less the money is worth in present day terms. Why do you think this is?

■ The net present value method

With most investments, there is an initial **outflow** of cash. This could be buying a machine, modernising a workplace, or simply buying new premises.

Then follows an **inflow** of cash. This can be increased profits, or reduced overheads.

To see if an investment is worthwhile, we need to compare the **inflows** (or benefits) with the **initial outflow** (or cost).

However, as we have seen, having an inflow of cash in, say, four years' time is not worth as much in present day terms.

We therefore need to **discount** future inflows of cash, to enable us to compare the figures.

A simple example will help illustrate this.

A firm decides to invest in a new plant. The initial cost is £5000. The estimated savings are as follows:

Year 1   £2000
Year 2   £2500
Year 3   £2500

The interest rate is 16 per cent, and the discount factors are:

Year 1   0.862
Year 2   0.743
Year 3   0.641

Is the investment worthwhile?

Solution:

Cash outflow £5000   Cash inflow:

	Year 1	£2000 × 0.862	= 1724.00
	Year 2	£2500 × 0.743	= 1857.50
	Year 3	£2500 × 0.641	= 1602.50
£5000		Total inflow	= £5184.00

Net inflow = £5184 – £5000 = + £184

The investment is worthwhile, therefore, as there is a net cash inflow: we get back £5184 in 'today's money'.

■ The cost of capital

The term 'interest rate' can mean many different things in business. When it is announced on the news that the government have cut (or raised) interest rates, a figure is usually quoted. If this figure was 6 per cent, does this mean that you can borrow from a bank at 6 per cent interest? Alternatively, will you be paid 6 per cent interest on your building society account?

In practice, you may find you only receive 3 per cent interest on your building society account, and yet are charged 16 per cent for borrowing from a bank!

ACTIVITY

How can you explain the difference in these interest rates?

PC 1
PC 2
AN 3.3

To allow for the fact that there is no single interest rate, businesses use **cost of capital** as a measure against which to assess the worth of an investment. An example is given below:

A business is deciding whether to buy new machinery, using net present value method.

- Interest rates set by the government are 6.5 per cent.
- The money for the machinery could be invested elsewhere, and earn 12 per cent (this is an example of **opportunity cost**).
- It will cost the business 17 per cent to borrow the money from a bank.
- It is quite risky investing in the new machinery.

The **cost of capital** will need to take all these factors into account. If it costs 17 per cent to borrow the money, the cost of capital needs to be **at least 17 per cent**! (Otherwise, the business pays out more in interest than it gains from the new machinery.)

Furthermore, if it is a risky venture, the owners will want more money back. The cost of capital will therefore be higher to reflect this.

(To understand this last point, consider betting on horses. The riskier the horse, the higher the odds and the more you win back if it is successful.)

In the above example, the business may choose a cost of capital of around 20 per cent. Unless the investment earns enough to cover this, it is not worthwhile.

In summary, cost of capital is an interest rate which reflects the risk of an investment project, together with the opportunity cost and cost of borrowing.

AN 3.3

ACTIVITY

Which interest rate discount factor table should be used when the cost of capital is 20 per cent?

PC 1
PC 2

Advantages of net present value method

- It takes into account future profits. Unlike the payback method, it does not ignore money that is earned by the investment after it has broken even.

- It takes into account the 'time value' of money. This helps a business avoid putting money into a project with insufficient returns.

Disadvantages of the net present value method
- It assumes that the interest rate/cost of capital remains constant through the life of the investment. This is clearly not very realistic – think how many times the interest rates have changed over the last few years!
- By taking into consideration cash inflows several years in the future, there is more chance of making false predictions. It is difficult for any business to accurately predict costs and revenues so far ahead.
- The net present value method assumes that all cash inflows occur on the last day of each year. In practice, of course, the cash comes in throughout the year. This is only a minor criticism, but it can make quite a difference where the interest rate is very high.

The Internal Rate of Return (IRR) method

Internal Rate of Return is another investment appraisal method that uses discounted cash flow techniques. It is similar to the net present value method in calculation. The net present value method simply states if there is a net cash inflow. The Internal Rate of Return method goes one stage further. It estimates the interest rate (or cost of capital) at which there is no net inflow or outflow of cash.

It is best to illustrate this by referring to a previous example:

A firm decides to invest in a new plant. The initial cost is £5000. The estimated savings are as follows:
  Year 1   £2000
  Year 2   £2500
  Year 3   £2500

The initial stage is to calculate the net present value using two different interest rates:

One interest rate which shows a *net inflow of cash*
Another interest rate showing a *net outflow of cash*

We have already calculated this for 16 per cent interest rate, and this shows a net cash inflow:

Cash outflow £5000   Cash inflow:

                              Year 1   £2000 × 0.862 = £1724
                              Year 2   £2500 × 0.743 = £1857.50
                              Year 3   £2500 × 0.641 = £1602.50

                   £5000   Total inflow   = £5184

Net inflow = £5184 − £5000 = + £184

Table of factors for the present value of £1

Year	11%	12%	14%	16%	20%
1	0.901	0.893	0.877	0.862	0.833
2	0.812	0.797	0.769	0.743	0.694
3	0.731	0.712	0.675	0.641	0.579
4	0.659	0.636	0.592	0.552	0.482
5	0.594	0.567	0.519	0.476	0.402

The next stage is to calculate a net present value which shows a net cash **outflow**:

Using 20 per cent as an interest rate:

Cash outflow £5000   Cash inflow:

                              Year 1   £2000 × 0.833 = £1666
                              Year 2   £2500 × 0.694 = £1735
                              Year 3   £2500 × 0.579 = £1447.50

                   £5000   Total inflow   = £4848.50

Net inflow = £4848.50 − £5000 = − £151.50

As the net inflow figure is negative, there is a net **outflow** of cash.

The point at which cash inflow exactly equals cash outflow occurs somewhere between 16 per cent and 20 per cent.

To calculate exactly where:

Add net cash inflow to net cash outflow (ignore negative signs):
    £184 + £151.50 = £335.50

This is divided by the change in interest rate:

$$\frac{£335.50}{(20\% - 16\%)} = £335.50/4 = £83.90 \text{ (approx.)}$$

This represents a fall of £83.90 in net cash inflow for each 1 per cent increase in the interest rate.

At 16 per cent, there is a net cash inflow of £184. Therefore, the point at which this becomes zero is:

16% + £184/83.90
=16% + 2.2% (to one decimal place)
=18.2%

Therefore, the Internal Rate of Return for this investment is 18.2 per cent.

What this figure means is that the investment is worth going ahead with if the cost of capital is less than this. If it is less, then there will be a net cash inflow.

The advantage of the Internal Rate of Return method is that it is possible to tell at a glance what the return on the investment is. This can then be compared with the cost of capital.

■ Using investment appraisal techniques in decision making

PC 3

As we have seen, the four methods each have their own advantages and disadvantages. Managers need to be aware of this when making a decision. In practice, the different methods may give conflicting advice. For example, of two machines, one may have a quicker payback period but a lower net present value than the other machine.

In such a situation, the manager must decide what the business's priorities are. If the business has a shortage of ready cash (or even a cashflow problem), then more weight may be placed upon a quick payback period. If, on the other hand, the business is thinking about a long-term investment, then net present value or Internal Rate of Return is of more use.

Furthermore, all figures of future returns are estimates, and the manager needs to decide how reliable these estimates are. If the business is a rapidly changing one, it may be impossible to accurately forecast several years ahead.

ACTIVITY

Which investment appraisal technique is likely to be most useful to a rapidly changing business?

SUMMARY

1 The four main methods of investment appraisal are: payback period; Accounting Rate of Return; net present value; Internal Rate of Return.

2 The payback period method calculates how long an investment takes to pay for itself. It ignores profits made after this.

3 Accounting Rate of Return considers future profits as well, but both methods ignore the time value of money.

4 Money has a time value. Money received at some stage in the future is worth less in today's money.

5 Discount tables enable us to calculate what money received in the future is worth in today's money.

6 The cost of capital reflects interest rates and the degree of risk involved in the investment.

7 The net present value method discounts money received from an investment, and compares it to the initial investment cost.

8 The net present value method also takes into account future profits.

9 There is a risk in predicting so far ahead.

10 Internal Rate of Return also uses discounting techniques. It calculates the rate of return on a particular investment. This method has the advantage of allowing direct comparison with the cost of capital.

QUESTION

PC 1
PC 2
PC 3
AN 3.2
AN 3.3
C 3.2

Franklin Ltd is a parcel delivery company. There is a choice of two new vans to buy:

	Van A	Van B
Initial cost:	£12 000	£10 000
Estimated savings:		
Year 1	£4000	£2500
2	£3000	£2500
3	£3000	£2500
4	£3000	£2500
5	£0	£2500
Scrap value at end of year 5:	£500	£2200

Your task is to advise the company as to which van to purchase. To enable you to do this, you should calculate for each van:

(i)   payback period
(ii) Accounting Rate of Return
(iii) net present value

The cost of capital is 10 per cent.

Write your findings in the form of a report.

Element 11.4 Assignment

Baxdale PLC is a motorcycle manufacturer. To compete with the Japanese manufacturers, the company has embarked on an ambitious capital investment programme, automating several construction processes and increasing the quality of the finished product.

PC 1
PC 3
PC 4
AN 3.2
AN 3.3
C 3.2
C 3.3

Task 1

Baxdale PLC has the choice of renting two pieces of equipment to make a single component, for which the following figures are available:

Machine	A	B
Annual rental	£4000	£5000
Budgeted annual output	560	680

Variable costs per unit:	
Raw materials	£3
Labour	£4
Selling price per unit	£17

You have been asked by the senior cost accountant to calculate the break-even number of units, and the safety margin for each machine, and to provide recommendations as to which machine should be rented. You should explain how you have reached your recommendation.

PC 2
PC 3
PC 4
AN 3.2
AN 3.3
C 3.2

Task 2

For the following three machines, Baxdale PLC has no option to rent; the machines have to be bought outright.

There is a choice of three machines to buy.

You have to advise the management on which machine, if any, should be chosen for the modernisation programme.

The details of the three machines are as follows:

MACHINE A   £
Cost   105 000
Scrap value after 6 years   12 000
Increased profit:
   Yr 1   40 000
   Yr 2   40 000
   Yr 3   20 000
   Yr 4   20 000
   Yr 5   25 000
   Yr 6 (excluding scrap value)   25 000

MACHINE B   £
Cost   200 000
There is no scrap value
Increased profit:
   Yr 1   70 000
   Yr 2   70 000
   Yr 3   70 000
   Yr 4   30 000

MACHINE C   £
Cost   180 000
Scrap value after 5 years   5000
Increased profit:
   Yr 1   80 000
   Yr 2   80 000
   Yr 3   30 000
   Yr 4   30 000
   Yr 5 (excluding scrap value)   30 000

The cost of capital is 14 per cent, and the discount factors are as follows:

Yr 1	0.8772	Yr 4	0.5921
Yr 2	0.7695	Yr 5	0.5194
Yr 3	0.6750	Yr 6	0.4556

PC 1
PC 2
PC 3
PC 4
AN 3.2
C 3.1
C 3.2
C 3.3

Task 3

An alternative to making a component for one of their products is to buy in the component. The figures are:

	Making component
Direct materials	£6
Direct labour	£12
Share of fixed costs	£4
Unit cost	£22

The component can be bought in for £21.50.

Present the arguments for and against buying in the component at a management meeting.

Glossary

Absorption costing A costing technique which allocates a share of overheads to every unit produced.

Accounting Rate of Return (ARR) An investment appraisal technique which calculates the average profit made by an investment. It ignores discounting.

Activity-based costing A costing method which groups costs around Cost Drivers.

Activity level An estimate of how many units of output can be achieved.

AVCO A stock valuation method which calculates an average cost for the stock held at any one time.

Basis of apportionment The measure used to split overheads between products or departments.

Break-even analysis A technique which shows the level of sales of a single product needed to cover costs.

Break-even point The point at which contribution exactly covers fixed costs.

Budget A detailed plan for a future time period. It is expressed in numbers (usually pounds).

Budget committee A group of senior people responsible for preparing budgets.

Budget Controller The person with overall responsibility for preparing budgets.

Budget manager Someone with responsibility for a particular budget.

Budgetary control The process of ensuring budgets are kept to and adjusted where necessary.

Capacity An estimate of how well resources are likely to be used for production.

Cash Budget Also known as a Cash Flow Forecast. It predicts how much ready cash a business will have over the next year or longer.

Contribution The selling price less the variable cost(s) of a product.

Conversion Cost The money spent changing raw materials to finished goods.

Cost Centre   A collecting place for costs. Where used, all costs go to one of the organisations' cost centres.

Cost Driver   The reason for a number of costs arising. It is used in Activity-based Costing.

Cost-plus pricing   A pricing method where a guaranteed profit is paid in addition to costs.

Depreciation   An accounting technique which spreads the cost of a fixed asset over several accounting periods.

Direct Cost   A cost related to a particular product.

Discounted Cash Flow   The general name for a range of investment appraisal techniques which take account of the fact that money loses value over time.

FIFO   A method of valuing stock which assumes that the stock first bought is that sold first.

Fixed Cost   A cost that does not alter with level of output.

Flexible budget   A budget that takes into account varying levels of output.

Indirect Cost   A cost that can't be attributed just to one product.

Internal Rate of Return (IRR)   An investment appraisal technique which determines a percentage return for the investment, using discounting techniques.

Level of control   The degree of responsibility needed to carry out a particular task.

LIFO   A method of valuing stock which assumes that stock bought most recently is likely to be sold before old stock.

Limiting factor   Something which prevents the business from growing beyond a certain point, e.g. sales demand, available machine time.

Line of control   Shows who a staff member is responsible to within an organisation.

Loss leader   A product sold at a loss in order to attract customers.

Mark-up   A method of pricing where a percentage of the cost of the product is added on to give the selling price.

Marginal cost(ing)   A costing technique which looks at the extra cost of producing more of a product.

Mission Statement   A brief written description of the goals of an organisation

Net Present Value (NPV)   An investment appraisal technique which converts future cash flows into their present-day value to enable comparison.

Net Realisable Value The money received for selling stock, less any selling costs such as postage, packing or commission.

Non-linear costs Costs that don't increase at the same rate as output.

Opportunity Cost The cost of not doing something else with a resource. Pre-determined absorption rate.

Overheads (Usually) indirect costs occurred in a business.

Payback period An investment appraisal technique which looks at how long an investment takes to pay for itself.

Planning cycle This has three stages: preparing the plan, executing the plan, and monitoring it.

Prime Cost The total of direct costs.

Replacement Cost The estimated cost of replacing all existing stock at current prices.

Revenue Centre A collecting place for money coming in to an organisation. *See* **Cost Centre**.

Safety margin The difference between forecast sales and the break-even number of sales.

Sales Value The level of sales, expressed in money received.

Sales Volume The level of sales expressed in number of units sold.

SSAP 9 A rule governing how published accounts must be presented. It affects several areas of cost accounting.

Standard Cost(ing) An estimated (budgeted) unit cost. Standard costing is a costing method using standard costs.

Step Cost A cost that increases in occasional 'jumps', rather than gradually, with output.

Strategic Plan A long-term plan which determines the development of an organisation over several years.

Sunk Cost A cost that has already been incurred, and is ignored in future decisions.

Unit Cost The cost of producing or buying one unit of a product.

Variable Cost A cost that changes with level of output.

Variance Analysis Comparing actual performance against budgeted or standard performance. The difference between budgeted and actual is a variance.

Zero-based budgeting A budgeting method that ignores previous budgets when preparing a new budget.

Appendix

Present value of £1 received

	2%	4%	6%	8%	10%	12%	14%	16%	18%	20%
Year 1	0.980	0.961	0.943	0.926	0.909	0.893	0.877	0.862	0.847	0.833
Year 2	0.961	0.925	0.890	0.857	0.826	0.797	0.769	0.743	0.718	0.694
Year 3	0.942	0.889	0.840	0.794	0.751	0.712	0.675	0.641	0.609	0.579
Year 4	0.924	0.855	0.792	0.735	0.683	0.635	0.592	0.552	0.516	0.482
Year 5	0.906	0.822	0.747	0.681	0.621	0.567	0.519	0.476	0.437	0.402
Year 6	0.888	0.790	0.705	0.630	0.564	0.507	0.456	0.410	0.370	0.335
Year 7	0.871	0.760	0.665	0.513	0.513	0.452	0.400	0.354	0.314	0.279
Year 8	0.853	0.731	0.627	0.540	0.466	0.404	0.351	0.305	0.266	0.233

Index